at the pinnacle of GREATNESS

Copyright © 2024 by LaShawn Davis

Published by Dream Releaser Publications

All rights reserved. No portion of this book may be reproduced, stored in a retrieval system, or transmitted in any form or by any means—electronic, mechanical, photocopy, recording, scanning, or other—except for brief quotations in critical reviews or articles, without prior written permission of the author.

Scripture quotations marked AMP are taken from the Amplified® Bible (AMP), Copyright © 2015 by The Lockman Foundation. Used by permission. www.lockman.org | Scripture quotations marked CEV are from the Contemporary English Version Copyright © 1991, 1992, 1995 by American Bible Society. Used by Permission. | Scripture quotations marked ESV are from The ESV® Bible (The Holy Bible, English Standard Version®), copyright © 2001 by Crossway, a publishing ministry of Good News Publishers. Used by permission. All rights reserved. | Scripture quotations marked GNT are from the Good News Translation in Today's English Version—Second Edition Copyright © 1992 by American Bible Society. Used by Permission. | Scripture quotations marked NIV are taken from the Holy Bible, New International Version®, NIV®. Copyright © 1973, 1978, 1984, 2011 by Biblica, Inc.™ Used by permission of Zondervan. All rights reserved worldwide. www.zondervan.com. The "NIV" and "New International Version" are trademarks registered in the United States Patent and Trademark Office by Biblica, Inc.™ | Scripture quotations marked NKJV are taken from the New King James Version®. Copyright © 1982 by Thomas Nelson. Used by permission. All rights reserved.

For foreign and subsidiary rights, contact the author.

Cover design by Sara Young
Cover photo by: The HR Plug

ISBN: 978-1-962401-18-0   1 2 3 4 5 6 7 8 9 10

Printed in the United States of America

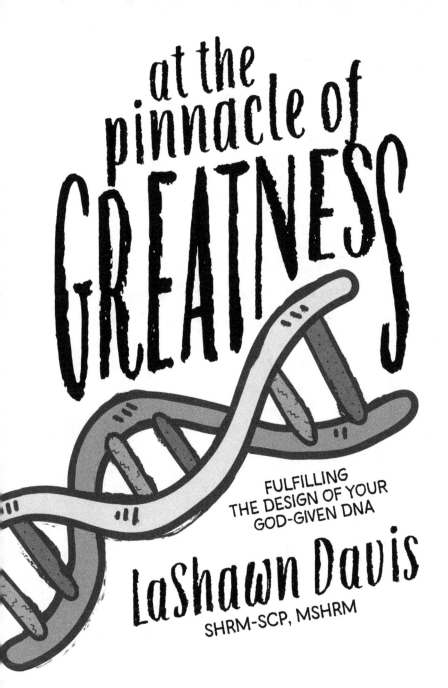

at the pinnacle of GREATNESS

FULFILLING
THE DESIGN OF YOUR
GOD-GIVEN DNA

LaShawn Davis
SHRM-SCP, MSHRM

DREAM
RELEASER
PUBLISHING

OTHER BOOKS BY LASHAWN DAVIS

*I Am Imperfectly Essential: Workplace
Declarations Affirming Your Value as Leaders*

To everyone searching for more, this book is for you. If you're holding this book, chances are you're seeking answers. You might be questioning your purpose, your place in this world, and how to find true fulfillment in life.

This book is for anyone who has ever felt lost or unsatisfied, who senses there's more to life than mere existence. It's written for those seeking not just to understand their path—but to walk it confidently.

Dedicated to your journey of self-discovery, these pages will not only guide and inspire you but also illuminate your path toward embodying greatness and realizing the grand design of your God-given DNA.

Welcome to your new beginning.

CONTENTS

ACKNOWLEDGMENTS

Thank You, Lord, for using me as a vessel for Your glory. To my husband, Victor, your unwavering support and love have been my anchor. I am so blessed to have you.

To my children, Nyla, Lea, and Cyan, thank you for your patience and understanding, sacrificing our time together to allow me the space to write.

To the two Dorothys in my life, who may not be with me on earth but are forever my guardian angels—your memory and influence remain a constant source of strength and inspiration. And, Teddy, Sandy, Jeffrey, Robin, and Paul, your constant love and presence in my life are invaluable. You have always been there, and for that, I am eternally grateful.

To my friends, who have walked this path with me, your encouragement and support have been invaluable.

And to those who doubted me, thank you. Your skepticism only fueled my faith and pushed me into a deeper discovery of my greatness. You inadvertently guided me toward this journey of self-realization, and for that, I am unexpectedly thankful.

INTRODUCTION

*W*elcome to a transformative exploration of your truest self in *At the Pinnacle of Greatness*. This book is more than a guide; it's a revelation that you are inherently Greatness, an expression of His divine excellence that is within you. Here, Greatness is not a distant goal but your distinguished identity, embedded in your DNA by God. This exploration is the key to living a life that transcends simple success to achieve true significance.

Embarking on this journey, you will delve into five key sections: **Identity**, where you'll embrace yourself as God sees you—as Greatness personified. **Mindset**, to fully comprehend and believe in your worthiness as greatness. **Vision**, where you'll reimagine your future embodying this greatness. **Strategy**, exploring how living as Greatness naturally attracts abundance and prosperity. And finally, **Legacy**, where your life, lived as Greatness, creates an enduring impact beyond your lifespan.

This book is an invitation to shift your perspective and live in the fullness of your God-given potential. You are not just striving for greatness; you are Greatness. Let this understanding illuminate your path as you turn each page, stepping into a life of purpose, power, and profound impact.

Welcome to a transformative realization: You are Greatness. This isn't a goal to achieve; it's a truth to embody, a reality woven into your very DNA by divine design. *At the Pinnacle of Greatness* is more than a book; it's a revelation that Greatness is your inherent identity, infused into your being by God.

IDENTITY

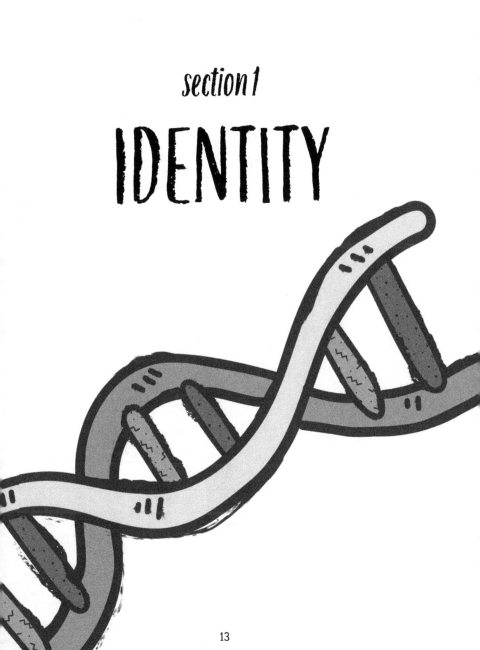

chapter 1

DISCOVER: YOU ARE GREATNESS

L es Brown, a widely recognized motivational speaker and accomplished author, has become synonymous with his inspiring speeches and teachings on personal growth, attaining success, and triumphing over adversity. Renowned for his profound impact, Les Brown has become an iconic figure, championing the empowering belief that "Greatness is Within You," a sentiment that he has become well known for, titled a book after, and incorporated as a part of his brand.

Not long ago, I found myself tuning into an interview featuring Les Brown, where he generously divulged his "7 Rules for Success." Throughout the conversation, he spoke with great wisdom about mindset, perseverance, and the endless potential we all possess. Each spoken word resonated deeply, leaving me with a renewed sense of inspiration and focus.

As Les Brown shared his fifth rule, "Greatness is Within You," during the thirteen-minute interview, I found myself chuckling, thinking, *Here we go again*. It wasn't that I was surprised by the statement—phrases like "Greatness Is Within Your Reach" or "The Journey to Greatness" have been bouncing around for ages. But in the momentum of that inspiring conversation, I kept an open mind, curious about Les Brown's unique perspective on this familiar concept. He said:

You have greatness in you. I don't know you, but here's what I know based upon my own experience: You have greatness in you. You have the ability to do more than you could ever begin to imagine. You have greatness in you. . . . You are different, you were created on purpose with a purpose to manifest that purpose through you. You were made in the likeness and image of God. Greater is He than he that's in the world. There's something in you that's greater than your circumstances. There's something in you that's greater than the adversities that you're facing. . . . You have greatness in you. That's my story, and I'm sticking to it.[1]

Let me be honest. There was a time when the idea of inner *greatness* wouldn't have caught my attention as much as it did on this day. It was life's unpredictable circumstances that had shoved me into a journey of self-discovery and introspection. It was my exhausting experiences in corporate America that forcibly drove me to rethink and, ultimately, change my outlook on my own identity. It was the experience of rejection, lack of acceptance, and the consuming battle of constantly having to prove my worth—despite consistently outperforming my peers—that led me to my breaking point. Knowing I was capable of more but unable to simply "do my job" caused me to reevaluate who I was, how I showed up, and why I was expected to prove my worth when others were not.

---

1   Les Brown, "7 Rules for Success," *Team Fearless*, January 11, 2018, video, 0:04:46, https://www.youtube.com/watch?v=Sdktvc1vKR8.

◇◇◇◇◇◇◇◇◇◇◇◇◇◇◇◇◇◇◇◇◇◇◇◇◇◇◇◇◇◇◇◇

It was my exhausting experiences in corporate America that forcibly drove me to rethink and, ultimately, change my outlook on my own identity.

I had nearly two decades of corporate experience and strong interviewing skills to a point where I could effortlessly secure roles perfectly tailored to my abilities. Once on board, I would deliver as promised, meeting and often exceeding expectations. My professional proficiency seemed to mirror precisely what each company claimed they needed. So why was it that I never managed to sustain any position for more than five years? My longest tenure capped at around 4.5 years and the shortest—nine months. What was going on? I had worked nine corporate jobs in eighteen years. Why did my professional journey consistently cycle from a point of acceptance and appreciation to a stage where I was perceived as a threat rather than an asset? Where was this "inner greatness," and why was it evading me?

REJECTION FROM THE WORKPLACE

I started researching and talking about my workplace woes with other colleagues and later learned I was not alone in my experience. There were several women who looked like me who also faced a lack of acceptance; their presence was unwelcome in the workplace. Being an employee—regardless of the level—is a consensual relationship between the individual and the employer. The individual decides to work there. The employer decides to hire them. It's the healthiness of the relationship that determines the experience for that individual. But relationships cannot be genuine when they are "built" around using a person for personal gain or a doctored image. So many companies were hiring Black women to check a diversity quota—hiring Black women because of our work ethic, ambition, and determination.

I ran across an article published by PositiveHire, sharing some interesting points that brilliantly captured what my workplace experience felt like. The article revealed how, for generations, Black parents have prepared their daughters to understand that they must be twice as smart, twice as independent, twice as talented, and simply "twice as good" to succeed in the face of racial discrimination.[2]

The article explained how in the United States, women are underrepresented at every level of the corporate ladder. Black women, despite often working "twice as hard," remain the most marginalized, lagging significantly behind both white men and women. According to the article, Black women "make up 13.7% of the U.S. population, yet they represent only 1.3% of senior management and executive roles of S&P 500 firms, 2.2% of Fortune 500 boards of directors, and there isn't a single black female CEO in the Fortune 500."[3] This is not merely an imbalance; it's an injustice. An injustice that continually causes Black women like me to have to fight simply to fit.

As I delved deeper into the article, a peculiar sense of comfort began to wash over me. It wasn't the comfort of delighting in the content but rather the realization that my experiences weren't isolated; I wasn't losing my mind. The data bore testament to my struggles, affirming the authenticity of my experiences. The author of the article, Michele Heyward, introduced a concept called "Intersectional Invisibility." Here's how she elaborated on it:

---

2 Michele Heyward, "Black Women Need To Be Twice As Good In Workplace," *PositiveHire*, positivehire.co/black-women-need-to-be-twice-as-good-in-workplace/.
3 Michele Heyward, "Black Women Need To Be Twice As Good In Workplace."

Ironically, Black women in workplaces are physically visible but cognitively invisible. The underrepresentation makes them stand out because they are the only 'one' in the room. But at the same time, they feel invisible because they are not seen for who they are, not heard for what they say, and not chosen for what they are good at.

They must adapt to this invisibility and work around various ways through which they can make their employers see them. When starting their careers, they have to be highly self-aware of when they are being noticed or ignored. When they move up the ladder a little, they have to intentionally take risky assignments to ensure their managers notice them. By the time (if) they are promoted to the executive position, they have to work hard to make sure they are not only performing their job but making a significant impact, so the organization can see them worthy of holding that position.

They are working multiple jobs in one designation. The original work responsibilities, the task of taking on challenges that no one else would take so they can prove their worth all the while scanning when they are visible or invisible to their bosses.[4]

Thissssss! I screamed in my head. This was me, my experiences. This is why I was tired. This is why I kept leaving job after job, trying to endure this cyclical trauma of workplace rejection that I couldn't figure out because I was only being me, working hard, and still being considered expendable.

---

4   Michele Heyward, "Black Women Need To Be Twice As Good In Workplace."

AN A-HA MOMENT

This took me back to a conversation a few months prior during a podcast episode I was hosting. My guest, a successful Black woman, shared a startling admission from a white executive. He confessed to hiring Black women for leadership roles within his company. This revelation was initially quite shocking, considering Black women are not typically the majority in corporate decision-making roles. But as the conversation continued, the stark reality behind his decision unfolded.

According to this executive, Black women tend to work harder than anyone else and will go beyond the call of duty without expecting additional compensation. In contrast, he observed that white women often couple their extra efforts with expectations for greater rewards, while white men prefer to delegate additional tasks, thus incurring extra resources. Essentially, the executive found that while white men prefer delegation and white women expect increased benefits, Black women often undertake more because of a deep-seated feeling of having something to prove.

The light bulb went off. As a Black woman, I was exploiting myself because of a subconscious belief that I had no other choice but to deliver exceptional performance. I had to volunteer for assignments outside of the scope of my job just to show them what I was capable of. I was driven by the natural instinct to have to prove myself, to demonstrate that I was just as competent and skilled as my counterparts. I constantly witnessed how when a white person commences a new role, it's generally assumed they possess the requisite qualifications and knowledge. In contrast, we, as Black women, often face immediate skepticism. It's as though we are constantly in the process of justifying our qualifications and experience, feeling perpetually stuck in a job interview: "What were you doing before you got here," often being the start of every new conversation.

As a Black woman attempting to succeed in the corporate world, it became critical for me to delve into the depths of my own identity and discover this "inner greatness" Les Brown eagerly expressed. As a Black woman, it was critical for me to understand my worth and recognize the great value I bring to every circumstance. It wasn't about my faults; I had enough of those against me, simply for being. No, I had to figure out what I had—that "they" needed—and flaunt it in front of them at every opportunity. I believed if I could figure out how to harness this hidden greatness, effectively use my unique gifts, and deliver value in authentic ways, I would be able to dictate my future on my terms, demand favorable working conditions most suitable for me, and end this cycle.

In the wake of this revelation, I made a firm commitment to strengthen and embrace who I am and discover this Greatness within me. So here's where I started: I enlisted the guidance of a mentor and a coach, drew wisdom and resilience from my daily Bible readings, amplified my prayer life, and dove headfirst into crafting a brand that authentically represented who I was. No more masquerading, no more imposter syndrome, no more attempting to mold myself, or conforming to the image I believed corporate America desired. Instead, I was going to embrace the identity that God designed for me and live the life I was created to live. I now had clarity on my assignment.

My encounter with this Les Brown interview was a search result from my quests for insights to unravel the intricacies of my self-discovery journey. The more I delved into this exploration, the clearer my understanding became of life's true essence and the power I held to shape its trajectory.

Previously, I might have willingly accepted the concept of this inner greatness dialogue, swept up in its seemingly logical and inspiring narrative. But my experiences, particularly in the corporate world, forced me to question these comforting ideologies that, while sounding appealing, did not seem to materialize in my own life. I was certain of my unique gifts and calling. I was guided by the affirmations instilled in me since childhood: "I am somebody," "I can become anything I set my mind to," and initially subscribing to the belief that "Greatness is within me." Yet, if these assertions were indeed true, why did I constantly encounter such disconcerting pushback from the world around me? As I delved deeper into understanding my identity, my perspective shifted, and I now wholeheartedly embrace the belief that I am Greatness. It's not something that is "within me." It is me; it's in my DNA.

◇◇◇◇◇◇◇◇◇◇◇◇◇◇◇◇◇◇◇◇◇◇◇◇◇◇◇◇◇◇◇◇

I wholeheartedly embrace the belief that I am Greatness. It's not something that is "within me." It is me; it's in my DNA.

FOUR POINTS OF DISCOVERY

1. GREATNESS IS NOT WITHIN YOU

Greatness is not merely a quality within you, nor is it something you need to actively seek or acquire. It is an inherent part of your being. You don't have to "step into" Greatness or go out to find it—it is an essential aspect of who we are.

My subsequent points will elaborate on this further, but first, I need to share a quick disclaimer. I know that Les Brown is not the sole advocate of this idea. Many books, quotes, and publications have expressed a similar sentiment, suggesting that Greatness resides "within" you. I mention Les Brown because he has incorporated this statement as a significant part of his personal brand. But again, he is not the only one who promotes this ideology. Many others also share similar beliefs when discussing or highlighting their thoughts on the concept of greatness.

I also want to be clear—I am not suggesting that Les Brown or anyone else who aligns with this viewpoint is wrong or mistaken in their beliefs. Everyone is entitled to their own thoughts and has the right to express them, just as those who agree with this idea do. We all have unique perspectives, and it is essential to respect the diversity of ideas. Okay, now that I've explained all of that, let's explore discovery point number two: why I hold a different outlook when it comes to this topic.

2. YOU WERE CREATED AS GREATNESS

Let's take a moment to think about the statement, "Greatness Is Within You." When we say something is "within" us, it can make us think that we could also be "without" it. So, to me, this statement implies that Greatness can be absent from us, which overlooks its true essence and the very way we are created.

This belief is rooted in the Bible, particularly in the book of Genesis. In Genesis 1:26 (AMP), it is written, "Then God said, 'Let Us (Father, Son, Holy Spirit) make man in Our image, according to Our likeness [not physical, but a spiritual personality and moral likeness].'" This verse reveals that we were created to reflect the spiritual and moral image of God Himself. We were intentionally designed, molded, and patterned after the very essence of God. Verse 27 (AMP) reinforces this truth by stating, "So God created man in His own image, in the image and likeness of God He created him; male and female He created them." Additionally, Job 33:12 (AMP) serves as a humbling reminder that "God is greater *and* far superior to man." This verse reminds us that, no matter how great we may perceive ourselves to be, God's Greatness exceeds ours infinitely. He stands as the ultimate embodiment of greatness, the epitome of excellence—He is the greatest.

To truly understand that we embody greatness, it's important to redefine how we perceive it. Because we were deliberately created and made in the likeness of a God who is the greatest, Greatness becomes an essential part of us by default, intricately woven into our very identity. It is a natural and inherent aspect of who we are, inseparably built into our core, a part of our DNA. Greatness is not something we acquire or develop; it is an innate quality of our being. Genesis 2:7 (NIV) tells us that "The Lord God formed a man from the dust of the ground and breathed into his nostrils the breath of life, and the man became a living being." It's His breath that we breathe. We are a part of Him, and He is a part of us. We were created as greatness.

3. YOUR GREATNESS REQUIRES CONNECTIVITY TO THE SOURCE

At the same time as grappling with the trials of workplace adversity, I was ensnared in a spiritual struggle. A deeply cherished relationship with my cousin, who was also the pastor of my church, shattered, resulting in me and my family leaving the church. The pain I experienced on all fronts was almost insurmountable, yet it ultimately proved necessary for my growth. If you're reading this and can relate to church hurt, family betrayal, or both, let me encourage you for a moment. I came to understand that God often disrupts our comfort when that comfort breeds complacency in our relationship with Him.

I had become so involved in ministry work that it consumed me. Between church-work, work-work, and homelife-work, I wasn't putting in any God-work. I had fallen into the trap of equating church activities with personal spiritual growth. I started to believe that the tasks I was doing, the services I was attending, and the outreach I was spearheading were enough to maintain my connection with God. But they weren't. The routine of going to church, I realized, is not synonymous with cultivating a relationship with God; it's merely a conduit. Church is like a bridge that takes you to the river but ultimately leaves you standing on the bank. The church, with all its rites and rituals, could bring me to the waters of spirituality, but it was up to me to dive in and swim.

Being "connected"—submerged—in the river is how your Greatness is ignited. I was into my life and my church but not into Him. I was busy doing the work but not fervently grounded in the Word. To make it plain, I had become too busy with doing God's "work" to put time into the work to build my relationship with God. What good can any resource be if you don't maintain connectedness with the source? Would it do you any good to use a water hose when it's disconnected from the spout?

Yes, I was doing the work of the Lord but based on what instruction? Based on whose instruction? I had not even consulted Him before making any moves. Jeremiah 29:11 (AMP) says, "'For I know the plans *and* thoughts that I have for you,' says the LORD, 'plans for peace *and* well-being and not for disaster, to give you a future and a hope.'" How would I come to understand His plan if I really didn't know Him? Despite all the "work" I was doing in the name of the Lord, it got to a point where I never stopped and asked the Lord, "Is this the work that you want me to do?"

I was operating solely from instruction from man, what looked good, and what felt right. I was operating on fumes, disconnected from the power source, receiving what little bit of juice I was getting from an extension cord through other people twice a week (Sundays for service and Wednesdays for teaching). What living being can absorb enough nutrition only by being fed twice a week? I was malnourished and dying. And, to save my life—although it hurt—the Lord allowed for this hurt to happen. It was necessary. It was at this moment I realized my feeling of emptiness resulted from people. Instead of finding fulfillment in Christ, I had hope built on man. And we all know that man will fail you, but God never fails. Your relationship with God is what fuels your ability to operate at the Pinnacle of Greatness. Yes, we are all Greatness—but living at the Pinnacle of Greatness offers an entirely transformed perspective on the essence of life.

◇◇◇◇◇◇◇◇◇◇◇◇◇◇◇◇◇◇◇◇◇◇◇◇◇◇◇◇◇◇◇◇

Yes, we are all Greatness—but living at the Pinnacle of Greatness offers an entirely transformed perspective on the essence of life.

4. COMPREHENSION OF YOUR GREATNESS PUTS AN END TO FEAR

The Bible leaves no room for ambiguity—suffering is part of being a disciple of Christ while living in this earthly existence. You must expect and accept there will be adversity when you commit to living as the Greatness of God, not because of who you are but because of whose you are. Consider Jesus's life—His Son. Living as an extension of Him, you must expect to face criticism, jealousy, discrediting, mockery, hatred, inquiries, and doubts—all things He encountered simply for being who God created Him to be.

In your journey, it's crucial to recognize that you are loved by God and have been handpicked for a distinct purpose (1 Peter 2:9). You've been bestowed with special spiritual gifts (1 Corinthians 12), set apart (1 John 2:20), and purposefully positioned in this life (John 15:16). Realize that you belong to Him. There is no need to seek approval from those who hold no authority over your life, for there is only one name, one authority that governs you.

Therefore, you must fear nothing of this world. As David boldly reminds us in Psalms 27:1 (ESV), "The Lord is my light and my salvation; whom shall I fear? The Lord is the stronghold of my life; of whom shall I be afraid?" As you strive to live a life that is pleasing to God, anticipate attacks from the enemy. The closer you get to embodying your true self, the more the enemy will strive to impede your progress. Not everyone will understand your assignment. So, you must not let the perceptions of others unduly influence you. Stand firm in your truth, guided by His light and love, and walk assuredly, knowing that you have nothing to fear.

YOUR SELF-DISCOVERY JOURNEY

It's time to jump into your journey of self-discovery. This journey may not always be straightforward or easy, but the reward—living the life you were divinely created for—is profoundly gratifying. Taking ownership of what genuinely belongs to you is crucial for your safeguarding and sustenance. Much like the intense affection and defense you extend to your children or anyone dear to you, that same fervor should be channeled toward guarding your own essence and identity.

Your identity is your possession, something intrinsically valuable that deserves your commitment and defense. You must be willing to fight for it, sacrifice for it, and invest in it because only when you recognize and appreciate your unique identity can you truly understand the level of power in your greatness.

Now is the time to fully embrace the profound truth that you are greatness! Greatness is something inherent, inseparable, and unremovable. It is knitted into your very DNA, eagerly waiting to be discovered, ignited, and unleashed. You must remember, Greatness is not an external pursuit or a competitive battle to fight; rather, it is a native part of your existence. It longs for your acknowledgment and genuine acceptance, eagerly anticipating the chance to manifest itself in all areas of your life.

◇◇◇◇◇◇◇◇◇◇◇◇◇◇◇◇◇◇◇◇◇◇◇◇◇◇◇◇◇◇◇◇◇◇

Greatness is something inherent, inseparable, and unremovable. It is knitted into your very DNA, eagerly waiting to be discovered, ignited, and unleashed.

You are God's masterpiece, His unique creation (Ephesians 2:10). He crafted and shaped you as an original edition that cannot be copied or duplicated. You are unlike anyone else. You were made in His image as a reflection of His greatness. Greatness is not just something you possess; it is who you are. So, walk with confidence as greatness. God's word is true and trustworthy, so choose to believe and receive it with your whole heart.

Whenever things get foggy and you need a moment of clarity, recite this special prayer as a reminder:

Thank You, Lord, for shaping me in Your image. In times of confusion and cloudiness, guide me toward clarity. When the fog of doubt tries to obscure my vision, brighten my path with the truth of your Word. Remind me of the incredible person you have created me to be. Please forgive my moments of self-doubt, when I've questioned those aspects of myself that the world has rejected or criticized. Help me to fully embrace who I am, knowing that You reside within me and stand by me. Strengthen me to stand firm in my identity, confidently, without fear. Remind me, Lord, that I am made in your image, fearfully and wonderfully designed. I am profoundly grateful for this unique journey You've set for me. I acknowledge that I am of royal lineage, and I wholeheartedly accept myself, even in the face of worldly rejection. For just as they rejected Jesus, I understand that seeking their validation is not my prerogative, for my life is dedicated to pleasing You alone. Amen.

chapter 2

EMBRACE: YOUR GREATNESS IS YOUR TRADEMARK

*D*r. Cindy Trimm is a renowned author, speaker, and empowerment coach known for her impactful teachings on spiritual growth, personal development, and leadership. She is recognized for her expertise in strategic prayer, spiritual warfare, and transformative thinking. I have the privilege of calling Dr. Trimm my mentor. She has guided me to recognize and overcome my limiting beliefs, self-doubt, and negative thought patterns, empowering me to unlock my full potential to achieve personal and professional success. Her wisdom and teachings have been undeniably life-changing while on my self-discovery journey.

Dr. Timm holds a profound viewpoint about identity. She once told me, "One of the most severe forms of betrayal, the utmost violence you can commit against yourself, and the most rudimentary aggression toward yourself, is to remain ignorant to who you are." These words serve as my powerful reminder of the significance of not just knowing my identity but the detrimental consequences of neglecting it.

WHO ARE YOU, REALLY?

What does identity mean? Why does it matter? We've already established that your identity is infused with greatness, a core element of every living entity that's part of God's creation. You may now be contemplating, *What's this Greatness that's an integral part of who I am?* Seriously, think about it. Have you ever found yourself asking, *Who am I, really?* Or perhaps, have you ever felt an overwhelming urge to disconnect, to seek isolation, because you needed time to genuinely "find yourself"?

Identity, in its most essential form, is about understanding who you are at your core, beyond societal labels or expectations. It's understanding the unique combination of experiences that make you, you. Identity is the framework through which you interpret and navigate the world around you. How you identify yourself influences how you engage with others, approach challenges, celebrate achievements, and make decisions that align with your values. Identity affects how you perceive and respond to life's most significant questions, triumphs, and tribulations.

◇◇◇◇◇◇◇◇◇◇◇◇◇◇◇◇◇◇◇◇◇◇◇◇◇◇◇◇◇◇◇

If you're finding yourself struggling to answer the question of Who am I? it's likely that you've been seeking answers in the wrong places.

When you find yourself asking, *Who am I, really?* it signifies a moment of introspection, a desire to understand your authentic self, untethered by external influences. Each one of us desires to uncover our identity, to grasp the essence of our existence, and to understand our unique purpose in life. This profound search, often expressed from varied paths, is a universal human experience. But if you're finding yourself struggling to answer the question of *Who am I?* it's likely that you've been seeking answers in the wrong places.

Let's imagine a scenario: You come from a long line of esteemed teachers. Your great-grandmother was a teacher, your grandmother was a teacher, and even your mother followed the same path. Naturally, everyone assumes that you will continue the tradition and become a teacher as well. Throughout your entire life, you are inundated with this expectation, and it becomes deeply ingrained in your mind. So subconsciously, you're wired to believe you're supposed to be a teacher, too.

But it's important to stop and think: Is this truly the path that aligns with your own inner calling and passions? Are you meant to follow in the footsteps of your lineage simply because it is expected of you? Is this who you were created to be? Without a clear understanding of your purpose and identity, it becomes all too easy to succumb to the pressures and expectations imposed by others. You may be very confident that a career in education is not for you. However, how can you effectively express your actual calling if you lack knowledge of what it is? Recognizing who or what you are not is not the same as having an in-depth awareness of who you are and the unique purpose you are destined to fulfill.

Remember, authentic self-discovery isn't about becoming who others say we are. It's about embarking on a journey inward, toward the essence of who we truly are and why we are here. When we try to fit into a mold created by external voices, we may lose our way, leading to a distorted perception of ourselves. Remember, your purpose and identity are inherently yours to discover, not for others to dictate.

It is all too common to find ourselves on paths defined by others, living out narratives and identities prescribed by society. We seem to base our existence on others' expectations, making decisions anchored in societal trends and the illusion of prestige. This self-abandonment manifests as we live lives that are anything but authentic, hiding behind masks of untruths, pretending to relish what brings us no joy solely for the purpose of social acceptance or respect. We often end up lost in roles that don't feel like our own, chasing dreams that don't belong to us. Often, such a masquerade isn't genuinely living—it's merely existing.

LIFE IS FOR LIVING, NOT EXISTING

Countless people are just existing in this world, living as strangers to their true selves. They inhabit their bodies like shells, their decisions dictated by what's been customary for much of their lives: wake up, work, eat, sleep, and repeat. This cycle becomes their daily routine until their last breath. But what I've learned is that this doesn't translate to truly living. Life isn't a static ritual or repetitive pattern to be mindlessly followed each day.

Indeed, simply "existing" rather than consciously and purposefully living can lead to a sense of disconnect and dissatisfaction. People might feel lost or stuck in their lives, often leading to a desire to "find themselves" or embark on a "soul search." This disconnect can manifest itself in various aspects of life, from whom we marry to our professional careers, where the feeling of being stuck with a person or in a job causes considerable unhappiness and distress.

◇◇◇◇◇◇◇◇◇◇◇◇◇◇◇◇◇◇◇◇◇◇◇◇◇◇◇◇◇◇◇◇

Living a life that aligns with your identity and intrinsic worth is about more than mere existence; it's about vibrancy, fulfillment, and purpose.

Living a life that aligns with your identity and intrinsic worth is about more than mere existence; it's about vibrancy, fulfillment, and purpose. It involves embracing your authentic self, nurturing your passions, and cultivating meaningful relationships and experiences. It's about setting and striving toward personal goals that resonate with your values rather than conforming to societal expectations. And most importantly, it's about recognizing and celebrating your Greatness and using it as a guiding force in your journey of self-discovery and self-fulfillment.

The journey of self-discovery is a fundamental step toward breaking free from the monotony of everyday life and stepping into a life of intention and purpose. Self-discovery involves diving deep into the essence of who you are—your identity, values, strengths, and areas of brilliance and genius. It's about uncovering and understanding your unique attributes and how they align with your purpose and aspirations.

This book will take you on the process of self-discovery, helping you formulate your own "life formula"—a personalized blueprint of how to live life in a way that honors your true self and allows you to realize your full potential by embracing your God-given DNA. This formula provides a roadmap full of equations that, once solved, will guide you toward becoming the best version of yourself.

So, think of self-discovery not just as a journey but a continuous, transformative process that shapes and enriches your life journey, that begins with knowing who you are.

HOW DO I DISCOVER MY IDENTITY?

The process of discovering who you are is a simple equation that will take some digging to complete. The first part of the equation is understanding your *Organic Brilliance*.

YOUR ORGANIC BRILLIANCE IS NATURAL

Organic Brilliance is the rawest form of authenticity. It refers to the talents, abilities, or knowledge that emerge naturally from you. It's not something that's learned or forced but a strength that blooms effortlessly from what's inside of you. This form of brilliance is unique to every person and reflects their individuality. It is activated from the intuitive thoughts or behaviors that come easily and naturally—actions that set you apart in a distinguishable way.

LeBron James is an example of someone who manufactured a life from his Organic Brilliance. LeBron is an American professional athlete, widely considered one of the greatest all-around basketball players of all time. During his junior year of high school, he appeared on the cover of *Sports Illustrated* magazine, where he was labeled as "The Chosen One." And before playing his first professional basketball game, he signed an unprecedented $90 million endorsement contract with the Nike shoe company.

The *Bleacher Report* published an opinion article written about James describing his distinctive abilities. A summary of the article stated these points:

LeBron James is widely regarded as one of the most gifted athletes in basketball history, transcending the game with his extraordinary skills, adaptability, and commitment to team success. This statement does not stem from an overstatement but from a recognition of his remarkable attributes that seem to challenge human norms.

While many associate Greatness with success, it's vital to understand that it actually originates from natural-born talent. In LeBron's case, his natural talent, honed by relentless hard work, combined with his imposing physicality, sets him apart from other basketball players throughout NBA history.

This screams Organic Brilliance! It is LeBron James's Organic Brilliance that sets him apart from being just another basketball player to being widely considered one of the greatest of all time. No one taught LeBron how to be this or do this; these results and reactions stem from his Organic Brilliance, his rawest authentic form of self. When you truly harness and hone your Organic Brilliance, your accomplishments become an integral part of your identity. They make you uniquely recognizable, leaving a lasting impression on others.

For instance, if you were to ask a random sampling of people who don't follow basketball if they know who LeBron James is, the chances are high that they would know exactly who he is. The reason is simple. When you invest time and effort into refining your Organic Brilliance, you inadvertently set yourself apart. There's no escaping who you're meant to be, and your distinctiveness shines in ways that most people don't understand. Absolutely, one of the remarkable aspects of Organic

Brilliance is its universal recognition. When you're operating in your natural element, it is almost impossible not to catch the attention of others in and outside of your industry.

LeBron James is a shining example of someone who discovered and nurtured his Organic Brilliance from a very early age. His exceptional athletic talent was evident even in childhood, manifesting at an age when such skills typically have yet to mature. This is a hallmark of Organic Brilliance—it's often an area where you've exhibited precocious ability or a natural inclination that's been with you for as long as you can recall. Reflect on your own life and consider those areas where your talent shone through effortlessly, regardless of age or circumstances. This could be a signal pointing to your very own Organic Brilliance.

DISCOVERING YOUR ORGANIC BRILLIANCE

Identifying your Organic Brilliance calls for deep introspection, unfiltered honesty, and complete authenticity. It's about taking a profound and truthful look at your abilities, talents, and passions that may have been evident from a very young age. When a child has the ability to create a symphony or solve advanced mathematical equations far beyond their years, this is indicative of Organic Brilliance at work. Each one of us possesses this exceptional talent or capability. It's a rooted aspect of who we are, and it often becomes most noticeable during our youth.

◇◇◇◇◇◇◇◇◇◇◇◇◇◇◇◇◇◇◇◇◇◇◇◇◇◇◇◇◇◇◇◇

Identifying your Organic Brilliance calls for deep introspection, unfiltered honesty, and complete authenticity.

To get started in your self-discovery quest, reflect on these ideas:
◇ Where does your Organic Brilliance live? Is it in music, mathematics, art, science, or maybe entertainment?
◇ What exceptional talents or abilities do you naturally possess?
◇ What have you been good at doing for as long as you can remember?
◇ Where have people complimented you for demonstrating extraordinary talent, particularly from a young age?
◇ What do people ask you for advice about?
◇ Whom do you admire? Where does their Organic Brilliance live? What are they known for? What do you admire most about them?

Leveraging your Organic Brilliance is the basis that will allow you to navigate life on your own terms. Fully understanding and tapping into this inborn genius side of you demands consistently fine-tuning and developing it to elevate to a level of mastery. This may entail enlisting the help of a coach, investing ample time for practice, undergoing training, or finding creative means to continuously sharpen your skill. Organic Brilliance is not just about raw talent; it also involves intense focus to perfect it.

YOUR INIMITABLE IMPRINTS MAKE YOU MEMORABLE
Once you take your Organic Brilliance and blend it with your *Inimitable Imprints*, you will have a clear understanding of who you are. Inimitable Imprints serve as the second part of the equation. They are memorable markings that carry a strong connotation of individuality and uniqueness. Let's break it down into a simple explanation by first dissecting the phrase.

Inimitable means something so unique and distinct that it can't be duplicated or copied. It's a one-of-a-kind feature or aspect. Imprints are marks or impressions that are left by an impact or influence. They are enduring and long-lasting, a sign of something that has substantial notability and can be considered a unique identifier.

Putting the two words together in this context, Inimitable Imprints could be defined as the unique and unrepeatable marks or characteristics that an individual has. They're the traits, behaviors, and responses that are uniquely yours and can't be copied or duplicated by others. These are the qualities that make you memorable.

◇◇◇◇◇◇◇◇◇◇◇◇◇◇◇◇◇◇◇◇◇◇◇◇◇◇◇◇◇

Everyone has Inimitable Imprints—
these are what make us distinctive and
add to our personal uniqueness.

Everyone has Inimitable Imprints—these are what make us distinctive and add to our personal uniqueness. Think of Inimitable Imprints as the elements that are impressionable, setting you apart from the crowd—the way you present yourself, your unique voice, behavior, and how you respond—the distinct qualities that contribute to your memorability and make you truly stand out. Unlike Organic Brilliance, Inimitable Imprints are less about your inherent abilities and more about the unique ways you present yourself to the world.

WHY MY HAIR IS PINK

My pink hair serves as an Inimitable Imprint, a distinguishable marker of my individuality. Deepening my understanding of my identity, I felt a growing urge to let others see the confidence I held in my own self-worth. When I decided to take responsibility and embark on this path of self-discovery, my goal was simple: to discover my own identity, embrace it totally, and fearlessly share it with the world. I made a commitment to brand myself truthfully and unapologetically, ensuring that whenever people encountered me, they would recognize my Greatness and understand the essence of who I am.

My experiences in corporate America illuminated the fact that lacking self-awareness leaves ample room for others to shape your narrative and construct plausible perceptions about you. I grew tired of others forming judgments based on their prejudice against Black women, drawing certain conclusions about who I was or what I could become merely based on the color of my skin or the texture of my hair. It was crucial for me to seize control over my own narrative and prevent external misinterpretations from defining who I truly was.

To celebrate this turning point, I took a daring leap by dyeing my hair various vibrant shades of pink. It stood as a visible testament to my pledge to embrace my true self and embark on my new path of self-expression and liberation. I am bold, audacious, bright, and colorful. This exudes in my personality, attire, decor—everything I naturally gravitate toward is bright and vibrant. So, despite my role as a senior leader in corporate America, I dyed my hair pink as a symbol of my blossoming self-assuredness.

My pink hair, while not a natural feature, has become a significant part of my identity. It sparks conversations and helps distinguish me from countless other HR practitioners. It's a distinctive marker that many associate with me. The frequent comment I hear is, "I knew that was you because of the pink hair." My pink hair has become one of my Inimitable Imprints—something unique and memorable that leaves a lasting impression on others.

Embracing authenticity means shedding all pretenses, including practices like code-switching. If my pink hair was a confidence booster outside of work, it was going to accompany me to work as well. I rejected the idea of conforming to societal norms or adjusting myself to fit into preconceived molds. Possessing a strong sense of self grants a fresh degree of freedom—the liberty to function and depart on your own terms.

Leveraging my Organic Brilliance and accentuating my Inimitable Imprints catalyzed a major shift in my corporate standing. No longer was I an interchangeable diversity hire but an irreplaceable asset. By simply being me and positioning myself in roles tailored to my strengths, I found my path to becoming unparalleled in my niche of workplace culture. My journey of self-discovery taught me how to become an indispensable asset. When you become indispensable, you have created such immense value that the organization would significantly suffer in your absence. The organization grows to rely on your expertise and contributions to such an extent that their need for you surpasses your need for them.

This reliance becomes visible when they proactively approach you with promotional opportunities, create new positions tailor-made for you, or offer substantial retention bonuses to keep you within their ranks. At this point, surface-level aspects such as your hairstyle, texture, color, piercings, or visible tattoos fade into insignificance. The value you bring to the table overshadows these superficial judgments.

The goal is to let your uniqueness shine through, not in spite of your Inimitable Imprints and Organic Brilliance but because of them. They are a crucial part of your identity and contribute to the unique value that you bring to your organization. Identifying and owning your Inimitable Imprints is a powerful way to express your identity and distinguish yourself from others. It's a part of your personal brand, and it can help you stand out and be remembered in an impactful way.

DISCOVERING YOUR INIMITABLE IMPRINTS

Let's start thinking about your Inimitable Imprints. For instance, if you are always dressed in bright, bold colors, that could be one of your Inimitable Imprints. I went to high school with a girl named Melissa. Throughout those years, and even into college, she was unmistakable in her choice of vibrantly bold prints and patterns. Fast-forward to today: she's an esteemed artist who has channeled her passion for art into crafting her own distinctive pieces and building a thriving business and brand. To this day, her signature prints remain her unmistakable trademark.

Perhaps you have a distinctive laugh that is unmistakable once heard. Or you might be known for your thoughtful, eloquent way of storytelling, causing others to listen intently whenever you speak. Your Inimitable Imprints are not limited to physical characteristics. They also encompass your behaviors, attitudes, or even the way you treat others. These unique attributes are an integral part of your identity. They shape how you are perceived by others and how you stand out from the crowd. To discover your Inimitable Imprints, start by asking yourself questions.

WHAT'S NOTICEABLE?

When people see you, before you say a word, what's one of the first things they notice about you? Think about when you meet someone for the first time; what do they generally make remarks about? What are the physical characteristics about you that are unique, distinct, and often discussed?

Cindy Crawford's beauty mark is a perfect example of an Inimitable Imprint. Instead of seeing it as a flaw or an imperfection, she embraced it and turned it into a signature aspect of her look. It's a unique feature that helped distinguish her from other models and added to her unique beauty. Just like Crawford, your Inimitable Imprints are distinctive features that set you apart from others. They are integral parts of your identity, and by acknowledging and embracing them, you can use them to bolster your self-confidence and personal brand.

WHAT'S QUOTABLE?

A phrase or term that you're known for or that people associate with you is another kind of Inimitable Imprint. A person's words can become a defining part of their identity and a major part of their Inimitable Imprint. Thought leaders are well-known for making statements in speeches, writings, or in the media realm that they become known for. Dr. Martin Luther King Jr.'s "I Have a Dream" speech is a perfect example of this. The speech has become synonymous with his name, and it is a key part of how people remember him.

What have you said, been quoted for, and been quoted about? What words or phrases have you "made up" that make sense when you hear it that people often repeat or use? What came from your genius or being that has left imprints in the minds or hearts of others? This kind of Inimitable Imprint could come in many forms. It could be a catchphrase that you always use, a term that you've coined, or even a specific way that you say or express something. The key is that people connect it with you when they hear or see it.

WHAT'S MEMORABLE?

Memorable actions or gestures can become defining features of an individual's identity. Just like words and physical characteristics, these actions can distinguish an individual from others and serve as a reminder of their unique personality or beliefs.

Did you do something that is forever ingrained in the minds of those who experienced it? Did you make waves for standing your ground on a matter that you refused to back down about? For instance, there were two remarkable athletes, Caitlin Clark and Angel Reese, who found themselves at the center of a compelling narrative in the world of college athletics. During the 2023 college basketball championship playoff, Caitlin Clark, a white player, drew attention with her playful rendition of John Cena's "You Can't See Me" hand gesture. The media raved about her act, branding it a fun and lighthearted twist to the high-stakes competition.

However, when Angel Reese, a Black player, echoed this gesture in a subsequent game upon winning the championship, the reaction was starkly different. Instead of applause, Reese was met with scorn. Her identical act was branded as "classless," and she was derogatorily referred to as an "idiot." The glaring discrepancy in reactions sparked controversy as spectators emphasized the revealing commentary was evidence of the racial bias that continues to persist in our society. A harmless gesture celebrated when performed by a white athlete was immediately demonized when replicated by a Black athlete.

The controversy surrounding Reese's actions, while initially negative, had an unexpected positive effect. Reese's decision to stand her ground and not be deterred from who she was amidst the backlash made her a memorable figure in women's college basketball. Her visibility skyrocketed, and so did her market value. This incident led to a significant increase in her name, image, and likeness (NIL) valuation, turning a challenging situation into a memorable career-defining opportunity.

Reese's story stands as a powerful testament to resilience and authenticity. Her story is a perfect illustration of how embracing your identity can inspire confidence and resolve. By refusing to hide your true self and displaying your unique characteristics, you, too, can create Inimitable Imprints. As shown in Reese's case, they can lead to memorable actions that spark discussions, leave a lasting impression, and even influence your reputation. Just remember, when expressing your authentic self, not everyone will understand or appreciate it immediately. You may encounter misunderstandings or misinterpretations, but it's essential to remain true to who you are and your beliefs.

How have your actions impacted the lives of others? What have you done, not with an intent to gain fame or notoriety, that inadvertently sparked positive controversy?

WHAT'S SOCIABLE?

Dieunerst Collin's experience serves as a quintessential illustration of how unplanned moments can pave the way for unforeseen recognition. Someone captured Collin's distinct expression and shared it on social media. This photo subsequently transformed into a meme that people would use to show feelings of confusion or discomfort. This unique visual signature became his Inimitable Imprint, making him an internet sensation and easily recognizable across digital platforms.

The spontaneous video taken of Collin at the Popeyes restaurant not only made him internet-famous but also created a long-lasting connection between him and the brand. In an interesting twist of fate, it led to a sponsorship deal with Popeyes 10 years later, demonstrating how digital culture and social media can play a significant role in shaping a person's identity, brand, and notoriety.

Are there particular types of social media posts you share that receive a lot of traction? Or, has someone used your name, image, or likeness to strengthen their position on a matter you may have been connected to? Using social media analytics can be a powerful tool in understanding the imprints lingering out there and if there's a digital persona tied to your identity.

◇◇◇◇◇◇◇◇◇◇◇◇◇◇◇◇◇◇◇◇◇◇◇◇◇◇◇◇◇◇◇◇◇◇◇◇◇

Remember, the process of self-discovery is not about creating a persona or trying to be someone else. It's about discovering who you are and learning to love yourself—just as you are.

Your Inimitable Imprints are not created intentionally or out of a desire to be memorable. They are naturally occurring, intrinsic elements of who you are. They are the unique traits, behaviors, and characteristics that set you apart from others and make you distinct. In fact, the examples given earlier—the Popeyes Meme Kid, Angel Reese, Cindy Crawford, and others—became memorable not because they tried to create a persona or alter who they were but because they were just being their natural selves. Remember, the process of self-discovery is not about creating a persona or trying to be someone else. It's about discovering who you are and learning to love yourself— just as you are.

Overall, figuring out your Organic Brilliance and Inimitable Imprints can be an exciting and enlightening journey. As you tackle the exercises to take deeper dives into introspection, consider these points:

◇   Self-reflection: Spend time reflecting on your life, your experiences, and your reactions to them. Try to understand what makes you, you. Reflect on what brings you joy, what you naturally excel at, and what feels authentic to you.

◇ Seek feedback: Ask for input from those who know you well. Friends, family, and colleagues may be able to provide insights into what makes you unique. Ask them to share their observations about your strengths, your unique qualities, and what they believe sets you apart.

◇ Journaling: Journaling can be an effective way to explore your thoughts, feelings, and experiences in depth. Over time, patterns may emerge that highlight your unique qualities.

◇ Recognize your values: What principles or beliefs do you hold dear? Your values are often reflected in your actions and decisions, making them a part of your unique imprint.

◇ Track your achievements: Look at your achievements, big and small. How did you achieve them? What unique skills or qualities did you use? Do you notice trends or patterns reflected in your achievements?

Understanding your Organic Brilliance and identifying your Inimitable Imprints is the foundational step of the self-discovery process. Completing this step will help acknowledge your special gifts and qualities that are a part of your unique design. Recognizing your Organic Brilliance will empower you to develop and utilize your natural talents to their fullest potential while embracing your Inimitable Imprints allows you to confidently express your authentic self to the world.

chapter 3

DISTINGUISH: YOUR GREATNESS REQUIRES "EMBRANDING"

*H*ave you ever realized how ketchup stands out among its fellow condiments? Think about mustard with its varieties: there's spicy mustard, honey mustard, Dijon mustard, and so on. Or even mayonnaise with its health-conscious alternatives like avocado oil, olive oil, or even Miracle Whip, which some prefer as a mayonnaise substitute. BBQ sauce goes even further with honey BBQ, hot brown sugar BBQ, sweet BBQ sauce, hickory BBQ, and countless other flavors. Yet, when we think about ketchup, its essence remains largely unaltered. Sure, there might be organic ketchup or sugar-free ketchup, but those aren't actual variations. They are simply ingredient substitutions. The fundamental flavor profile of ketchup remains constant, as does its distinct identity as a condiment.

This analogy relates to you as an individual. You are like ketchup—not in the ordinary sense but in a peculiar, insightful way. In this vast grocery store we call life, individuals often feel pressured to shift and shape their identities to match societal expectations or trends, much like the competing flavors of mustard or mayonnaise. However, like ketchup, your core identity maintains a distinct, unaltered flavor; there aren't any variations of you. Sure, there can be growth and change, like ketchup's sugar-free or organic alternatives, but these are facets of your development, not fundamental changes to who you are. Although you will evolve and mature, the core of your designed uniqueness will always remain unchanged.

KETCHUP ON BROCCOLI?

In our quest for self-discovery and embracing our identity, we find parallels in the most unlikely of places. Ketchup, a seemingly mundane condiment, perfectly illustrates this concept. Though there are no variations in its ingredients, ketchup is still very versatile. Its universal appeal comes from its ability to enhance the flavors of a multitude of dishes, from French fries to scrambled eggs and beyond.

My friend has a son, and when he was around three years old, he was picky when it came to trying new foods. She discovered a clever workaround: she would tell him that whatever unfamiliar food was on his plate was "just like chicken nuggets," a food he already knew and loved. Convinced by this comparison, he was more comfortable trying new things. But there was a catch: he had to put ketchup on it because that's what he did with chicken nuggets. She found her son putting ketchup on things most wouldn't dream of, such as broccoli, eggs, and mashed potatoes—but that was his thing, and the ketchup additive worked for him.

This story emphasizes the point that even though ketchup remains consistent in its nature, its role can vary significantly depending on its need. Despite its varied preferences, the substance of ketchup remains unchanging. Think of your distinguished identity in terms of ketchup. Just as ketchup holds its own unique and reliable taste amidst a multitude of condiments, you, too, stand distinct in this diverse world—without a need to adjust to suit the tastes of others. It's all about consistency, authenticity, and versatility.

◇◇◇◇◇◇◇◇◇◇◇◇◇◇◇◇◇◇◇◇◇◇◇◇◇◇◇◇◇◇

No matter where you are or who you're interacting with, your core—your greatness, your Organic Brilliance, and your Inimitable Imprints—remains uncompromisable. It's what makes you uniquely you.

No matter where you are or who you're interacting with, your core—your greatness, your Organic Brilliance, and your Inimitable Imprints—remains uncompromisable. It's what makes you uniquely you. Not everyone will choose you as their preferred option, but those who do will appreciate and value your unique flavor of contributions. We're all humans, fundamentally the same, yet each with our own unique twist—our distinguished identity. Some people will like us, some will love us, and some may prefer us only in specific circumstances or combinations. That's all part of the richness of human diversity. Embrace your unique attributes, your "ketchup-ness," if you will, as they are what make you stand out and resonate with the people you are purposed for.

THE STARTING POINT

Defining your organic brilliance is more than just a self-discovery exercise; it serves as the foundation, or starting point, to establishing your personal brand. If you overlook this step, you may find yourself on a far more complex and laborious path to success than necessary. Without this fundamental understanding, you risk wasting valuable hours, if not years, artificially living in an identity that does not authentically reflect who you are.

Your personal brand is an unapologetic affirmation of your true self. This brand remains consistent, regardless of the situation or setting. There's no need to adjust, pretend, or code-switch based on your audience. It's purely, authentically being you, always. Altering your natural demeanor to appease others is not only exhausting but also counterproductive. Constantly adapting to external expectations drains you of your energy, while celebrating your genuine self will fill you with confidence and pride. Operating in your authentic design magnetically draws those who resonate with your story, talents, and time, rendering irrelevant those who don't. There's no energy consumed on trying to fit into someone else's box. Instead, you shine brilliantly, standing tall unboxed in your God-given DNA.

The truth is, your organic brilliance lies at the heart of your brand identity. Once you discover it, you will gain a clear vision of what you have to offer and how you can bring value to others. With this knowledge, your branding journey becomes more straightforward, meaningful, and successful. And then it's your inimitable imprints that serve as the bow on the package, making you discoverable within the crowded marketplace.

YOUR BRAND IS THE PRIORITY

There's a deep-rooted notion suggesting that the moment a business idea springs to life, the first step should be to brand it. This perspective encourages immediate action to design your logo, decide on colors, register a business name, launch a website, initiate a social media presence, and then craft an inventive marketing strategy to attract customers. Yet, as widespread and sensible as this might sound, it's essentially flawed.

◇◇◇◇◇◇◇◇◇◇◇◇◇◇◇◇◇◇◇◇◇◇◇◇◇◇◇◇◇◇◇◇◇

Understand who you truly are, discern your core values, and recognize your distinct value proposition. With clarity on these facets, your business will mirror these attributes.

It's often simpler to brand a business because articulating what we enjoy doing comes more naturally than defining who we truly are. But before diving into branding your business, it's paramount to first focus on understanding and refining your personal brand. Understand who you truly are, discern your core values, and recognize your distinct value proposition. With clarity on these facets, your business will mirror these attributes. As you journey deeper into this path of self-awareness, you'll realize that a business is essentially an extension of you. Let me share my personal journey to illustrate this point more vividly.

YOU: THE BRAND BEFORE THE BUSINESS

Back in 2016, I knew I wanted to establish myself in the HR consulting space. I started with a concept called HR Refresh, aiming to infuse a refreshed perspective into the image of HR. So, I followed the "standard procedure"—formed an LLC, designed a logo, built a website, and began to publicize my new venture.

However, it wasn't long before I was swamped with requests for resume writing. At first, I was fine with writing them, but as time went on, it felt less like a fulfilling task and more like a recurring frustration. As I worked on writing resumes, I couldn't shake the feeling that so many people were targeting careers that were not in sync with their true potential. It was as though I had a clear vision of their talents being better utilized elsewhere. And although I tried to steer our conversations toward other possible avenues to explore, their focus remained fixed on simply securing that next job.

During that period, I overlooked these intuitive nudges—subtle signals from my organic brilliance, urging me to pivot from the complacency and unfulfillment of what I was doing. But, despite the evident unsettledness, I kept going, believing the forward momentum would lead to more business generation. So, even with my diminishing passion, I continued with resume writing to sustain the business. Ironically, I was mirroring the very actions of the job seekers I was advising; I was settling for what seemed necessary simply because it paid the bills.

Fast-forward to 2019, I had enough and decided to rebrand and came up with my current company: The HR Plug. This time, my concept was to be the connection—or "the plug"—for career and business HR needs. I deliberately did not offer resume writing services but focused on offering advice and guidance for workplace issues. I would still get several people contacting me about offering generic HR services for their small business, something I "could" do but knew I wasn't "called" to do.

But for the sake of business, I did this for a while and again realized I still wasn't feeling complete. Something was missing. I was working and generating income, but I wasn't finding fulfillment. I wanted to do more than just advise; I wanted to problem-solve and customize actual solutions. So, for the third time in five years, I went through another rebranding process. But this time, I kept the name The HR Plug, and focused solely on improving workplace culture and experiences. My offer became specific—to help businesses strategize people solutions, support disengaged employees, and improve the overall workplace experience.

This process of trial and error, of rebranding and reassessments, was a costly journey to discovering the real essence of my personal brand. What I learned was that every iteration of my business reflected my evolving understanding of myself and my true passions. I wasn't just trying to build a business; I was branding myself—to ultimately reflect who I was and what I wanted to offer through my business. It was only after realizing *I was a brand* that I would find that sense of fulfillment, giving me the energy and desire to scale and grow my business.

◇◇◇◇◇◇◇◇◇◇◇◇◇◇◇◇◇◇◇◇◇◇◇◇◇◇◇◇◇◇◇◇

It was only after realizing I was a brand that I would find that sense of fulfillment, giving me the energy and desire to scale and grow my business.

DISCOVERING THE DEPTHS: NOT ALL STEAK IS CREATED EQUAL

Many people catch a glimpse of their purpose and, upon feeling that initial spark of joy, prematurely conclude they've discovered their true path. It's like deciding to try steak for the first time and ordering it from Steak 'n Shake. After relishing that burger, you might assume that's the finest steak because it was new and enjoyable. So, every time you crave a good steak, you go back to Steak 'n Shake because it's all you know. Having tasted it just once, you're now under the presumption that you've savored the very best of what steak has to offer.

But this is where the danger lies: in premature contentment. For me, the realm of HR was my Steak 'n Shake. I've always enjoyed roles that allow me to find and amplify the hidden potential in others. Naturally, this steered me toward a career in HR. Here was an industry with a simple premise that deeply resonated with me: helping people and organizations thrive. So, I convinced myself that if I were operating within the confines of HR, I would fulfill my true calling. But settling for just being in the purview of HR is no different than accepting a Steak 'n Shake burger as the epitome of steak. You've tasted something good, and it's tempting to stop there, thinking you've found the best. But in doing so, you'd be overlooking the deeper, more refined cuts and flavors awaiting you at elite steakhouses like Capital Grille. While Steak and Shake serves steak and satisfies a basic craving, it's not the pinnacle of what steak can offer in terms of flavor, quality, and experience.

This steak journey mirrors the path many individuals tread in their professional lives. They uncover a talent or passion, experience a taste of success or fulfillment in a particular area, and then settle there, thinking they've reached the peak of their potential. But just like in our steak analogy, there's often so much more depth, richness, and potential waiting to be explored. If we remain content with the initial taste of our passions, we risk missing out on the richness that specialization offers. We settle for a Steak-and-Shake moment—a taste of alignment and the temptation to remain there.

It's essential to challenge the boundaries of our initial discoveries. Too often, we find something we're good at, something that feels right, and we camp there. But what if there's more? What if, just beyond that initial realm of comfort and competence, lies a specialty, a niche, an avenue that aligns so perfectly with our organic brilliance that work feels less like duty and more like destiny?

I urge you not to cap your journey at mere discovery. Delve deeper. If I had settled at just the surface level of HR, I might still be drafting resumes, convincing myself that it was my ultimate calling simply because it felt right. But work isn't just work, much like steak isn't just steak. It's about finding that unique intersection where your Organic Brilliance aligns with what you do daily.

◇◇◇◇◇◇◇◇◇◇◇◇◇◇◇◇◇◇◇◇◇◇◇◇◇◇◇◇◇◇

Work isn't just work, much like steak isn't just steak. It's about finding that unique intersection where your Organic Brilliance aligns with what you do daily.

YOUR BRILLIANCE IS YOUR BRAND

No matter what you do, whether for a company or your business, it should resonate with your Organic Brilliance. In my case, part of my

Organic Brilliance is being solution-oriented. I have a natural ability to rapidly identify problems, pinpoint what isn't working, and rearrange it so it does. When I was writing resumes, I wasn't providing solutions for job seekers, I was simply exacerbating the problem by helping them find jobs that I knew would lead to further discontent down the road. As I worked to brand myself and dig deeper, I learned that it's the problem-solving components of HR that come as natural to me as breathing, making it feel less like work and more like fulfilling my purpose. This became clear when people asked, "How did you know what to do?" or "How did you see this in me?" I often struggle to answer simply because it's my natural ability to do it—it's my Organic Brilliance.

Another piece of my Organic Brilliance is my ability as an insightful visionary. Instead of offering generic fixes, I craft tailored solutions that ignite greatness. This inspires individuals to discover their passions and urges businesses to cultivate environments where people can freely manifest greatness. I've come to understand that regardless of the domain I'm in when I'm leveraging this talent—igniting Greatness in individuals and organizations—it never feels burdensome. Instead, it resonates with my innate calling. That's the foundation upon which I've built my brand: The Greatness Guru.

And just as I am greatness, so are you. We all have been crafted by the same hands, stemming from the same Creator. My purpose is realized when I guide you to uncover your inherent greatness, aligning your life with His divine design. As Ephesians 2:10 (AMP) states:

> *For we are His workmanship [His own master work, a work of art], created in Chris Jesus [reborn from above—spiritually transformed, renewed, ready to be used] for good works, which God prepared [for us] beforehand [taking paths which*

He set], so that we would walk in them [living the good life which He prearranged and made ready for us].

This scripture underscores the very essence of my mission; I am here to guide you in understanding and fulfilling your divine life plan, to help you grasp how your unique, God-given DNA is intended to manifest in your life.

EMBRANDING 101: EMBRACING MEETS BRANDING

Embracing and projecting our true identities—what I like to call "Embranding"—is a transformative process that brings us closer to our divinely-appointed purpose. Embranding is a term I created to signify the fusion of "embracing" with "branding." While it may not yet grace the pages of dictionaries, in my book, it should! Embranding is the intentional act of fully accepting, understanding, and showcasing your distinguished identity. It's about wearing your authenticity with pride and making it a central pillar of your brand's message.

◇◇◇◇◇◇◇◇◇◇◇◇◇◇◇◇◇◇◇◇◇◇◇◇◇◇◇◇◇◇◇◇

Embranding is the intentional act of fully accepting, understanding, and showcasing your distinguished identity.

By authentically representing who we are, we step into the path God has meticulously designed for each of us. As stated in 1 Peter 2:9 (AMP):

But you are a chosen race, a royal priesthood, a consecrated nation, a [special] people for God's own possession, so that you may proclaim the excellencies [the wonderful deeds and virtues and perfections] of Him who called you out of darkness into His marvelous light.

This scripture highlights our unique standing and purpose in God's grand design. By embranding ourselves, we not only acknowledge our divine heritage but also position ourselves to walk fully in the blessings and promises of our Creator.

BUSINESS FORMATION STARTS HERE

My story is a testament to the truth that our unique gifts and talents are an essential part of our personal brand, and it's your personal brand that will align with everything else that you do in life—including your business. Think about Jay-Z's famous quote: "I'm not a businessman, I'm a business, man." I've now come to grasp its profound significance: I, as an individual, am the business. Any logos, websites, and business names—they're all secondary. At the heart of it all, both the brand and the business are intrinsically me, living out my purpose.

So, if you don't fully know yourself, how can any business you create be truly representative of you? How can you extend or manifest anything meaningful and sustainable? Without this foundational self-awareness, there's a perilous cycle of rebranding, relaunching, and restless searching. Only by truly discovering and embranding can there be a clear path to finding purpose—a purpose that, once realized, ensures genuine fulfillment and success.

People often drift without purpose because they lack mental clarity. Many are unaware of their true selves, much less their desired purpose and destinations. However, once you understand precisely who you are and how you wish to embrand that essence into a realized purpose, your path becomes much clearer. From then on, every action, every business endeavor, and every decision will propel you in a direction congruent with your identity.

Now that you understand this, study your Organic Brilliance and Inimitable Imprints and ask yourself: *What do I want to do with my unique identifiers? In what ways can I brand my distinguished identity to reflect my divine design?* Discovering and embranding your identity is the first step; the next is to build a brand so unmistakable that everything you produce is identifiable, thrives, and seamlessly associated with you.

We'll revisit the concept of business as an income generator later in chapter 12, but for now, the key point to remember is this: You don't need to hire a brand strategist or embark on a branding process as the initial steps for establishing your business. As a matter of fact, before you even entertain the idea of a business, you should focus on comprehending your greatness, understanding your identity, and embranding your personal brand as your distinguished identity.

chapter 4

CLARIFY: YOUR GREATNESS DEMANDS CLEAR ARTICULATION

*T*he business landscape is currently facing what I call an identity crisis. Driven by an aspiration to replicate the success of others, numerous entrepreneurs overlook the essential journey of self-discovery. Instead, they adopt strategies, copycat approaches, and even purchase courses that offer the secrets to scale a business to six or seven figures. They believe that this route is the expressway to success. The result is a market convoluted with competition, a whirlwind of businesses and people striving to mirror what they benchmark as accomplishment, creating a highly competitive environment that's essentially a battlefield of replicas.

This problem is significantly compounded by another prevalent issue—the blurred lines between identity, assignment, and social status. In today's world, many people classify their sense of self directly to their job titles, how well business is doing, or their standing in society. Identity isn't about ranks or scales. Just because you have a high-ranking job doesn't make you more valuable than someone in an entry-level position. Your job title is about your assigned duties, not your worth as a person. Similarly, the success of your business doesn't define your value, and neither does how well-known or respected you are in society. Everyone is equal in the grand scheme of things; we all were created in the likeness and image of God. When we start believing these superficial things make us better than others, it creates unnecessary division of classism. It's not uncommon to see individuals struggling to describe themselves without instinctively mentioning their job title, accomplishments, or proud achievements. Yet, these things, as impressive as they might be, aren't the crux of your identity. It's this mistaken belief in a hierarchy of worth that causes problems and misunderstandings among people.

◇◇◇◇◇◇◇◇◇◇◇◇◇◇◇◇◇◇◇◇◇◇◇◇◇◇◇◇◇◇◇◇

Failing to embrand your Organic Brilliance and carve your unique path is effectively neglecting yourself, overlooking God's design for you, and ultimately sidelining your distinguished greatness.

This identity crisis is ultimately a disservice to everyone. It not only impacts the individuals who lose touch with their true selves but also creates a market saturated with clones rather than originals. The pressures of being accepted or fitting in have become so overwhelming that people have become confused about who they are or pretend to be someone they're truly not. This has led to a dangerous cycle of comparison and imitation, resulting in a dog-eat-dog society where individuality and authenticity are the casualties. Imitation is not the best form of flattery; it's actually self-betrayal. Failing to embrand your Organic Brilliance and carve your unique path is effectively neglecting yourself, overlooking God's design for you, and ultimately sidelining your distinguished greatness.

In Psalm 138:8 (AMP), David makes a heartfelt plea: "The LORD will accomplish that which concerns me; Your [unwavering] loving-kindness, O LORD, endures forever—Do not abandon the works of Your own hands." This speaks to moments when we, too, call upon God, asking Him to remember us in our times of need. But who are we asking Him to remember? An imitation of someone else or the genuine "us" He uniquely crafted? Recognizing that we are the works of His hands means we must earnestly pursue His plan for us and live as His designed masterpiece.

To truly align with His design and purpose requires a significant mindset shift. We must reevaluate and adjust how we perceive and articulate our identities. If we desire God's intervention during the pivotal moments in our lives, it's imperative that we think about who we are differently, aligning ourselves more closely with His vision for us. Only then can we resolve this identity crisis and create a society where authenticity and individuality are celebrated, not suppressed.

REDEFINING SELF: A MINDSET SHIFT

With the understanding that our identity is a fusion of our Organic Brilliance and Inimitable Imprints—culminating in our unique personal brand—it becomes crucial to adopt a refreshed mindset. There should be a level of clarity when we introduce ourselves and in all our interactions, ensuring that the description of who we are isn't overshadowed by mere superficial labels. To genuinely understand our calling, it's paramount that our mindset resonates with the divine designer. The words of Philippians 2:5 (NKJV) urge us, "Let this mind be in you which was also in Christ Jesus." This isn't merely about imitating behaviors or following commandments; this speaks to embracing Christ's perspective of us, acknowledging our worth and capabilities. As we strive to see ourselves through His eyes, we establish a life anchored in genuine self-awareness, authenticity, and purpose.

THE IDENTITY CRISIS REVEALED

It wasn't until the 2023 UNPLUG conference that I understood how alarming it was that so many people had lost touch with their genuine selves and the impact it was having on the workplace experience. Before I delve into the events of the 2023 conference, let me clarify the objective of this gathering. In 2022, I was the driving force behind the first-ever UNPLUG HR business conference. UNPLUG was born as a solution for an urgent need to address the overwhelming exhaustion and burnout that HR professionals were feeling because of the harsh circumstances the COVID-19 pandemic created for the labor environment. The chaotic conditions left HR professionals feeling underappreciated, underserved, under-compensated, and outright depleted. They were expected to take care of the needs of both workers and leaders, all while no one was taking care of them. Fresh data from LinkedIn underscored this concern. In 2022, HR recorded the highest turnover of all job functions worldwide, with an alarming quit rate of 15 percent, a stark contrast to the global average turnover rate of 11 percent. This proportionally meant HR's turnover was over 35 percent above the norm.[5]

As an HR professional myself, I saw the UNPLUG Conference as a transformative undertaking. It afforded HR professionals an opportunity to disconnect from the grueling corporate environment and unify within a supportive network of like-minded peers and colleagues. The conference was an important factor in reigniting their passion, revitalizing their spirits, and restoring their depleted energy resources. Realizing the significance of self-discovery, I wanted to share strategies that would give attendees the confidence to recognize and express their unique value, which would set them apart from others, leading to a heightened sense of fulfillment and a balanced state of wellness.

So, during the UNPLUG 2023 conference event, I facilitated an exercise aimed at assisting participants in writing a personal statement to memorialize and remind themselves of who they were—their distinguished identity. With all my newfound revelations swirling around in my head, I was so excited about what was about to unfold. I walked onto the stage, faced the audience, and with a big smile asked, "Who would be willing to step to the mic and answer this simple question for the group: Who are you?"

My huge smile was met with an awkward moment of silence, blank stares, bowed heads to avoid eye contact, and faces turning from left to right, looking around the room. It became poignantly clear that several individuals were struggling to answer this question. In that moment, it became evident to me: unless HR professionals could redefine and truly embrace their genuine selves, these industry struggles would persist. After a bit of convincing, there were a few brave souls who reluctantly decided to tackle a response, but instead of answering my question, they ended up reciting statements that sounded more like elevator pitches.

The discrepancy was evident: there was work to be done. I've since integrated a day into the UNPLUG Conference dedicated solely to personal introspection, well-being, and professional growth. This deviates from the norm, as most HR and business conferences prioritize business tactics rather than focusing on the individual needs of the practitioner. However, I was determined to bridge this gap, to illustrate the profound influence of individual identity on the overall health of businesses and organizations.

EMPOWERING AUTHENTICITY: A CORPORATE SOCIAL RESPONSIBILITY

It's vital to understand that the challenges corporations face with their business outcomes are directly linked to this identity crisis. The landscape has shifted: for businesses to thrive, employees now need more than just compensation—they need to feel seen, valued, and heard. People are not only expected to excel in their roles but also to put on a persona that might not align with their true selves. This constant act of performing both personally and professionally can be overwhelming. The resulting strain often drives individuals to either push back or resign, leading to operational disruptions for businesses.

The landscape has shifted: for businesses to thrive, employees now need more than just compensation— they need to feel seen, valued, and heard.

Fixing the identity crisis isn't just limited to the HR and business professionals' responsibility. There's an overarching corporate obligation at play here. It's high time organizations prioritize the well-being of their leaders and employees—not just as representatives of the company's brand but as humans with distinct identities and emotions. When individuals feel their contributions are overshadowed and their authentic selves suppressed, it begs the question: How can they genuinely serve, inspire, or lead?

Many corporations boast of prioritizing diversity and inclusion efforts. However, their efforts seldom transpire into anything more than an impactful position statement on their website. They say they value diversity yet institute dress codes that limit hair colors and styles and set arbitrary guidelines about beards, tattoos, and piercings—irrespective of whether these factors impact an individual's capacity to perform their job.

Companies must move past the narrow lens of "What's in it for us?" and look beyond mere spreadsheets and performance metrics—instead, appreciating and empowering the people driving their business success to be their genuine selves. In doing so, companies can foster a richer, more human-centric environment, emphasizing factors that truly influence performance outcomes rather than superficialities. When organizations begin to value their people for who they are—not just what they can do—it reintroduces humanity and emotion into the world of work. And that's precisely the paradigm shift that the conference seeks to catalyze, urging employers to genuinely practice what they preach by investing in their people as people first.

I realize it will take time for society to truly grasp the profound connection between personal identity, organizational health, and business success. Still, the challenge is worth the effort. If with each conference, we can inch these professionals closer to embranding their

Organic Brilliance and Inimitable Imprints, we can mitigate the loss of irreplaceable talent—those that hold the aptitude and solutions to redefine and invigorate the HR landscape.

And as I look ahead, I envision a future for the UNPLUG Conference—an optimistic prophecy. Five years from now, when I pose the same question to an audience that's quintupled in size, backed by corporate endorsements and overwhelming community support, I anticipate a distinct change. In this future, when asked about their identity, the response from HR professionals and business leaders will resonate with authenticity and self-awareness, free from rehearsed elevator pitches and pauses of uncertainty. Instead, the room will resonate with genuine reflections, a testament to the growth of not just the conference but of an entire professional community proudly embracing who they are.

ELEVATOR PITCHES VS. PERSONAL BRAND STATEMENTS

Elevator pitches and Personal Brand Statements serve distinct purposes and should not be used interchangeably. An elevator pitch is typically a concise, convincing summary sharing a product, idea, or information about you and what you do well. It generally lasts about thirty seconds to two minutes—the average duration of an elevator ride. Elevator pitches are geared toward promoting or selling something. They are primarily used in professional or networking settings to quickly capture someone's attention and generate interest. The objective of an elevator pitch is to make an impact that lasts and gets people interested or involved quickly.

During the exercise at the conference, I purposefully didn't ask for an elevator pitch. I didn't ask, "What do you do?" or "What are you good at?" or "What is your business all about?" I posed a straightforward question—three simple three-letter words: "Who are you?" Personally, I'm not a fan of elevator pitches. They make sense in the right settings I suppose, but the more I hear them used as a personal introduction, the more I can see how we are becoming a society that finds status and achievements more valuable than the traits and characteristics that define who we are. You can have a great "elevator pitch," and while I may understand **what** you're good at doing, I still have no idea **who** you really are. Look at this example of an elevator pitch of someone who is a retail manager:

Hello! I'm Taylor, a seasoned retail store manager with a passion for delivering exceptional customer experiences. With years of proficiency leading teams, optimizing operations, and driving sales growth, I specialize in creating a positive and engaging environment that both employees and customers love. By fostering a motivated and customer-centric team, I consistently exceed sales targets and enhance overall store performance. If you're seeking a dedicated manager who can elevate your retail operations to new heights, I'm here to make it happen.

Taylor sounds like a remarkable manager, doesn't she? Perhaps. But despite being well-acquainted with her professional accomplishments, expertise, and customer service approach, all I've received is an elevator pitch that fails to offer any genuine understanding of who she is. Elevator pitches focus more on the what—what you do, what you're good at, and what you offer.

On the other hand, there are what I like to call "Personal Brand Statements." A Personal Brand Statement is a type of introduction that focuses on telling people about your personal brand, values, and distinguishing characteristics; it introduces your distinguished brand identity. It is a concise and memorable summary of who you are, what you stand for, and the value you bring. Unlike elevator pitches, Personal Brand Statements can be more flexible in length and allow for a more comprehensive introduction of yourself.

◇◇◇◇◇◇◇◇◇◇◇◇◇◇◇◇◇◇◇◇◇◇◇◇◇◇◇◇◇◇◇◇◇

A Personal Brand Statement is a type of introduction that focuses on telling people about your personal brand, values, and distinguishing characteristics; it introduces your distinguished brand identity.

Caroline Wanga, the Chief Executive Officer (CEO) of Essence Ventures, offers a great example of a Personal Brand Statement on her LinkedIn profile. For those who don't know, LinkedIn is a professional networking site where people can connect, create professional relationships, and showcase their talents and experience to potential employers, clients, or individuals who choose to follow an influencer's account. If you search for "Caroline A. Wanga" on LinkedIn, click on her hyperlinked name, and navigate to her "About" section, you'll discover her skillful presentation of a Personal Brand Statement—a concise summary capturing her essence and providing insight into her identity. It reads:

> *I enjoy leading the transformation of organizational culture. I thrive in innovative environments. I define success by helping people get to their destination, their way. I manage*

teams by setting the destination and negotiating the many paths to get there. I model authenticity and fearlessness by first doing the things I ask others to do. I inspire action and self-empowerment by telling simple stories and pushing the boundaries of what can be accomplished. I celebrate risk-taking, and extract risk-learnings with a strategic lens and jovial spirit. I am a self-proclaimed cultural architect with particular passion for constructing, deconstructing, and reconstructing organizational culture.

Caroline Wanga's Personal Brand Statement effortlessly showcases her strength and character, eliminating the need to rely on job titles, work experience, accomplishments, or external validations. To put this in perspective, understand that Caroline certainly has bragging rights. She has a myriad of accomplishments under her belt. She's been heralded as the Top Executive in Corporate Diversity by Black Enterprise and lauded by Savoy as one of the Most Powerful Women in Corporate America. She is the co-founder of WangaWoman, an initiative dedicated to optimizing individual and organizational purposes. She is the Chief Executive Officer of ESSENCE Communications, Inc., the leading media, technology, and commerce entity for Black women. Before that, she made an impact at Target Corporation as the Chief Culture, Diversity, and Inclusion Officer. Nevertheless, when introducing herself, she set aside these significant milestones and chose authenticity over accolades, focusing on who she is, not just what she's achieved.

Personal Brand Statements do just that—focus more on the "who": who you are, whom you serve, and the unique value you bring. They are introductory statements that capture your identity, your target audience, and the authentic qualities that distinguish you, creating a powerful representative expressive statement about you.

WHY YOU NEED A PERSONAL BRAND STATEMENT

How do you go about defining who you are? When someone asks you the question, "Who are you?" do you find yourself emphasizing your occupation, achievements, or details about your business? In simpler terms, do you respond with phrases like "I'm an executive at . . ." or "I'm the owner of . . ."? Or, does how you describe yourself change based on who you're talking to? Does your answer change when you're in a business setting versus when you're with family and friends? Your response when telling people who you are should remain consistent, regardless of the audience. If you feel driven to change how you present yourself depending on who you're talking to, it suggests there could be a lack of authenticity in your life.

In our achievement-driven society, there's a pervasive belief that conformity is the key to success. But Caroline Wanga challenges this notion head-on with her powerful assertion: "If you can't be who you are where you are, you change where you are, not who you are."[6] This statement underscores a critical mindset shift we all must undertake. It's not about bending ourselves to fit into predefined molds but about reshaping environments that don't acknowledge or appreciate our greatness.

Perhaps you are finding yourself in a situation, like the UNPLUG HR business conference attendees, where you struggle to generate a meaningful response when asked who you are. Or, maybe up until now, you have linked your identity to job titles, accomplishments, or the expectations of others, allowing those factors to shape how you present yourself to the world. If any of these scenarios resonate

---

6   Bruce M. Anderson, "Stop Focusing on Retention, Says Essence CEO, and Aim for Something Much Bigger Instead," *LinkedIn*, 27 Oct. 2022, www.linkedin.com/business/talent/blog/talent-connect/stop-focusing-on-retention-says-essence-ceo-caroline-wanga.

with you, it could indicate a deeper underlying issue that warrants your attention.

It's imperative to establish a Personal Brand Statement that offers clear insight into who you are for both you and others. Stand firm in your truth, never wavering under the weight of others' standards. If they can't value who you are, it might be time to reconsider your environment. No one should stay where their worth isn't recognized and appreciated.

◇◇◇◇◇◇◇◇◇◇◇◇◇◇◇◇◇◇◇◇◇◇◇◇◇◇◇◇◇◇◇◇◇◇◇

If they can't value who you are, it might be time to reconsider your environment. No one should stay where their worth isn't recognized and appreciated.

BEING CLEAR ABOUT YOUR IDENTITY IS LOVING YOURSELF

Boldly embracing your identity is the epitome of self-love. In an age where achievements seemingly matter most, we must shift our mindset to recognize that truly loving ourselves transcends flaunting achievements—it's about audaciously showcasing who we inherently are. Our identity is not a sum of accolades but a reflection of our passions, values, beliefs, and unique intricacies—it's this uniqueness that forms our authentic brand. Genuine self-love arises when we cherish these elements rather than mere accomplishments. In this light, every act of showcasing our authentic self becomes an act of profound self-appreciation.

CRAFTING YOUR PERSONAL BRAND STATEMENT

It's time now to craft your Personal Brand Statement. By this point, you've identified your Organic Brilliance, those inherent gifts and talents that you naturally possess, and you should have also discerned your Inimitable Imprints, the distinct, memorable characteristics that visually represent you or create an impression about you based on what others have seen or heard. These two revelations combined define your identity, the essence of who you are. Your Personal Brand Statement will synthesize these components to form an introductory declaration about yourself.

Let's break down how to go about creating this pivotal statement:

STEP 1: TAKE A PERSONAL PERSPECTIVE

Begin your journey by diving deep into self-reflection. Start by identifying your core self, using simple nouns, asking: "Who am I?" Then, ponder on what fulfills you, your areas of Organic Brilliance, and your unique imprints. Describe yourself using five adjectives and consider the problems you're passionate about solving. Reflect on others' perceptions of you: what do they notice first, and what compliments do you frequently receive? Pinpoint moments of joy, confidence, and your proudest achievements, both personal and professional. Lastly, envision the legacy you want to leave behind. This introspection lays the foundation for crafting an authentic Personal Brand Statement.

STEP 2: TEST YOUR ASSUMPTIONS

After you've spent time in introspection, it's essential to seek external viewpoints. Engage with five trusted individuals, asking them specific questions to understand their perception of you. Dive into their initial impressions, areas they consider you an expert in, and the descriptive words they associate with you. Delve into their understanding of your unique qualities and tasks they'd rely on you for. Recollect their memories with you, from the first interaction to their most cherished moments. By juxtaposing their feedback with your self-assessment, you can pinpoint both alignment and possible discrepancies in how your personal brand is perceived.

STEP 3: PUT IT ALL TOGETHER

After gathering your self-reflections and the perceptions of others, begin a comparative analysis. Identify which descriptions about yourself align perfectly with others' perceptions. It's essential to pinpoint any discrepancies between your self-perception and how others see you. Were there characteristics or values you overlooked or perhaps emphasized too much? Reflect deeply on these gaps and the potential reasons behind them. Finally, determine which values and characteristics are frequently linked to you. Ponder whether these truly resonate with your own understanding and definition of your identity.

STEP 4: BEGIN CRAFTING YOUR STATEMENT

Reflect on your responses and identify a recurring theme or aspect that is unique to you. Use this to shape your Personal Brand Statement. Here's my Personal Brand Statement as a reference:

"I am LaShawn Davis, and I inspire greatness and success. I am the catalyst that propels individuals toward their highest potential."

Remember, this process isn't about crafting a perfect statement right away. It's about creating a foundation that authentically represents you and your value and refining it over time as you continue to grow and evolve.

STEP 5: REFLECT, REFINE, AND REVISIT

Crafting a Personal Brand Statement is an ongoing process that demands frequent reflection. Once you've outlined your statement, evaluate its resonance with your identity, ensuring it aligns with your Organic Brilliance, Inimitable Imprints, and others' perceptions of you. Rather than focusing solely on skills or titles, it should underscore "who" you are. Seek honest feedback from trusted peers, but remember that while feedback informs, it doesn't dictate. Refinement is about aligning more closely with your essence, not about altering your core identity. Once refined, embed your statement in all your professional touchpoints, from bios to networking interactions. However, remain adaptive—just as you evolve, your statement should too, reflecting your ever-growing personal and professional journey.

LET IT AFFIRM YOU

To make the most of your Personal Brand Statement, practice reciting it every day in front of the mirror until you remember it by heart. Words have great power and can deeply impact you and those around you. Let your Personal Brand Statement serve as a positive affirmation. The more you repeat positive affirmations, the more they become a natural part of your thinking, shaping your beliefs and actions. Doing this daily will lay the foundation for unlocking your full potential to operate in true greatness. And when you've successfully tapped into your esteemed greatness, you will position yourself as an unstoppable force, empowering you to pursue endeavors that resonate with your values, purpose, and personal development.

Remember to embrace who you are and the unique person God has created you to be. Remember that you are one-of-a-kind, uniquely fashioned with a special purpose that only you can fulfill. In a world that often encourages conformity, remember the special gift of your individuality. But just in case you ever forget who you are or find yourself lost in the noise of the world, take solace in the divine reminders scattered throughout the Bible.

IDENTITY PRAYER:

Lord, I know that I was not an accident. My very existence was planned as I was knit together and formed in my mother's womb (Psalms 139:13). Lord, You have complete knowledge of every intricate detail of me, even the number of hairs on my head (Matthew 10:30). Every detail of my life is planned, and I know You have plans for prosperity for my life. Plans for peace and well-being, and a hopeful future (Jeremiah 29:11).

I am chosen (1 Peter 2:9). I have been set apart, specially gifted, prepared (1 John 2:20), and called for a special purpose (1 Corinthians 12). I have been adopted, appointed, and purposefully planted (John 15:16) in this life.

I am fearfully and wonderfully made (Psalms 139:14); a bright light that cannot be hidden (Matthew 5:14). I am drenched with grace and favor (Ephesians 1:6) and crowned with love and mercies (Psalms 103:4).

I am a vessel who belongs to the highest (1 Corinthians 6:20). Lord, I am royalty, with immeasurable and unsurpassed riches of your grace (Ephesians 2:7). I am an heir of Christ's spiritual blessings, and though at times it may feel like suffering, I will endure and receive favor, and experience Your glory (Romans 8:17).

I am a new being, reborn and renewed, not weighed down or held hostage by my past mistakes. I am forgiven. I am redeemed (2 Corinthians 5:17-18). I am strong. I am infused with inner strength and confidence enabling me to succeed in all things (Philippians 4:13) aligned with your plan for my life.

God, You created me to be the head. I am a leader. I walk in integrity with honorable character and moral courage (Proverbs 2:7). I rise above and land on top (Deuteronomy 28:13). I have complete sufficiency in all things (2 Corinthians 9:8). Every one of my needs will always be supplied.

When I listen to Your voice God, and yield to Your instructions, I am overtaken by blessings. Your Word tells me in Deuteronomy 28 that my land, property, and possessions are blessed (Deuteronomy 28: 8). Wherever my feet trod, I am blessed (Deuteronomy 28:6), and simply because of who I am, my bloodline is blessed (Deuteronomy 28:4).

I am intellectually sound, operating with the mind of Christ (Romans 12:2) and an overflow of divine wisdom (Luke 2:52). My mind is righteous. You are fearless (Psalms 34:4) and far from oppression (Isaiah 54:14).

I am healed and whole, free from all sickness and disease (Isaiah 53:5; 1 Peter 2:24). I walk in supernatural immunity, where plagues, disease, and outbreaks cannot infiltrate my body (Psalm 91:10). I am redeemed from the curse of sin, sickness, and poverty (Deuteronomy 28:15-68; Galatians 3:13). Weapons formed against me will never prosper.

I am an unshakeable force, operating in this life, Lord, with Your strength and Your shield of protection (Psalm 28:7). I am a powerful authority over the enemy (Matthew 10:1). Evil cannot dwell in my vicinity because even it fears this power that fuels me.

I am entangled with your Holy Spirit, causing me to never be alone (1 Corinthians 6:19), abandoned, rejected, or forgotten (Hebrews 13:5). I am protected and always safe (Psalm 18:2) because I am born of you, and therefore untouchable by the enemy (1 John 5:18).

Lord, I am because You are, and it is You within me that is greater than any opposition I could face in this world (1 John 4:4). Even when I fail You, I am forgiven. I might even stumble, but I will not fall. I am more than a conqueror. I am victorious (Romans 8:37).

I am greatly loved by You (John 3:16; Ephesians 2:4; Colossians 3:12; 1 Thessalonians 1:4), and I live to please You (Philippians 3:14). I am Your masterpiece, Your workmanship (Ephesians 2:10), crafted and molded as an original edition that cannot be copied or duplicated.

Lord, I am created in Your likeness (Genesis 1:27) and Your image. I come from You, who are the greatest, which means I am Greatness. I realize that Greatness is who You say I am. So, forgive me, Lord, for the times that I fall short in allowing my identity to slip away from this frame of mind. Thank You for this revelation. Lord, I thank You for my life. Thank You for creating me. In Jesus's name. Amen.

Let this prayer serve as a reaffirmation of your unique and divinely crafted identity and a reminder that you have been made with purpose for a purpose. As you move forward, carry this understanding with you, let it form the foundation of your personal brand, and let it guide you as you make your unique mark on the world.

section 2:

MINDSET

chapter 5

COMPREHEND: YOUR GREATNESS DECLARES YOU WORTHY

Imagine being given a blank canvas, three primary colors—red, yellow, blue—and a brush, with the challenge of painting a beach. At first glance, the task seems daunting; traditional beach hues are absent. However, mindset makes the difference. A limited perspective sees only the obvious colors provided. In contrast, an expansive one delves into experimentation, producing sunsets with mixing colors to create shades of orange, lush foliage in green, and shadows in purple.

◇◇◇◇◇◇◇◇◇◇◇◇◇◇◇◇◇◇◇◇◇◇◇◇◇◇◇◇◇◇

Often, perceived limitations can hinder our potential, yet much like the vast array of shades that can emerge from three primary colors, our capabilities are boundless.

This scenario parallels life. Often, perceived limitations can hinder our potential, yet much like the vast array of shades that can emerge from three primary colors, our capabilities are boundless. It's not the external challenges but our mindset that truly determines our path. Comprehension of your esteemed Greatness allows you to access unparalleled destiny dimensions. Often, the most substantial barriers are mental rather than tangible. Remember, with the mindset of royalty—as a child of the King—you have the power to rise above perceived limitations and mold your unique narrative.

Remember the legendary encounter between David and Goliath (1 Samuel 17)? Goliath, a formidable giant, towered over the Israelites with a fearsome reputation and an imposing presence. His very name invoked terror, with a stature and combat record that made armies tremble. David, on the other hand, was but a young shepherd, seemingly ill-equipped and vastly outmatched.

Yet, David possessed something immeasurable—an unwavering mindset. If David had operated solely on what was immediately evident—the towering stature of Goliath, the giant's impressive record of victories, and the palpable fear he instilled in the Israelite army—he might have never mustered the courage to confront him. But David didn't allow the intimidating exterior of his adversary to overshadow his conviction. Instead, he adopted a mindset of victory because he trusted not in his own strength but in the divine power of God. He recognized that physical appearances were secondary to spiritual faith and resilience. With a sling, a stone, and his belief system, David defeated the giant that many deemed undefeatable. He demonstrated that having the right mindset can overcome even the most insurmountable odds.

Harnessing the power within, you have the remarkable ability to shape your fate through your mindset. As believers, it's paramount to recognize living in a world of sin requires mental discipline. Given the ever-present challenges from adversaries, 1 Peter 5:8 (ESV), "Be sober-minded; be watchful. Your adversary the devil prowls around like a roaring lion, seeking someone to devour," cautions us to stay vigilant. Our ultimate challenge is to gain control of our minds, a domain of immense value. The Bible counsels us to guard our thoughts, which stresses the spiritual warfare anticipated to take place within them. Consider 2 Corinthians 10:5 (AMP):

> *We are destroying sophisticated arguments and every exalted and proud thing that sets itself up against the [true] knowledge of God, and we are taking every thought and purpose captive to the obedience of Christ.*

As outlined above, our responsibility is to challenge thoughts that contradict God's teachings, steering them toward Christ's teachings and obedience. The adversary, ever so cunning, frequently attempts to infiltrate our minds with seeds of uncertainty, apprehension, and turmoil. Guided by Scripture, our mission is to scrutinize these intruding thoughts against Christ's message and redirect our mindset to align with His truth and wisdom.

MASTERING THE MIND WITH DIVINE PERSPECTIVE

Mindset Mastery requires combining your faith with God's promises and taking charge of thoughts that oppose His Word. This mastery over your mind enables you to guide your life not merely by what you observe physically but by what you believe spiritually. The more aligned you become with your divine purpose, the greater threat you pose to the enemy. So, it becomes imperative to maintain control over your thoughts and viewpoints. Mindset Mastery, a potent combination of spiritual discipline and mental strength, paves the way to fully embrace the life that God has carefully designed for you, fulfilling your divine destiny.

Mindset Mastery hinges on perspective—it's about directing your mind to view challenges as gateways to favorable outcomes, much like the artist who, with just three primary colors, envisions a vast spectrum of hues. Recall the painting analogy; mastering your mindset isn't about denying the limitations of the palette options or wishing for more colors. Instead, it's about embracing the tools you have and reshaping your viewpoint to create art despite the seeming constraints.

Just as an artist can manifest a beach scene with just red, blue, and yellow by blending primary colors to produce unexpected shades, you, too, can navigate life's challenges regardless of what it looks like you have or lack. It's not merely accepting the obstacle but rather fostering an inquisitive spirit, being curious about the lessons or insights God intends for us to derive from the circumstance.

◇◇◇◇◇◇◇◇◇◇◇◇◇◇◇◇◇◇◇◇◇◇◇◇◇◇◇◇◇◇◇◇◇◇

When a mountain presents itself in your path, it is not an obstacle but an affirmation of God's trust in your strength to conquer it.

Think about it this way: when a mountain presents itself in your path, it is not an obstacle but an affirmation of God's trust in your strength to conquer it. It is mental assaults and mind attacks, however, that can cause us to question this belief. This is because your thoughts also have a prophetic influence over your life. How we think forecasts and controls our actions and outcomes, thereby shaping the trajectory of our lives. As such, understanding and mastery over your mind is crucial in both affirming and upholding your greatness-infused identity. It's not sufficient to merely know this truth; you must genuinely believe it, let it permeate every aspect of your existence, and reflect in every action you undertake.

NURTURING THE MINDWOMB

Beyond the mind needing direction and guidance, it also requires vigilant care. Maintaining alignment with God's promises amid the enemy's unrelenting attacks requires tremendous mental stamina to avoid suffering mental exhaustion. So, it's not just about steering your thoughts but also nurturing them by providing a suitable environment conducive to maintaining self-regulated mental wellness and peace.

Your mind lives in a space that I call the "Mindwomb," a completely self-governed environment, acting as an external cradle for your belief systems. The Mindwomb concept illustrates our capacity to control our outcomes by determining the conditions that nurture our thoughts and beliefs. Consider the physical womb as an analogy. The womb provides a protective, nurturing, and sustaining environment necessary for a baby to grow, develop, and eventually make their way into the world. In a similar vein, the Mindwomb represents your internal environment that governs your mindset—it's the "space" where your beliefs about yourself, your perceptions of your self-worth, and your comprehension of your Greatness take shape and mature. Much like how a mother has the responsibility to create a conducive environment for her baby's healthy growth, it's also your responsibility to maintain an environment conducive to the healthy cultivation of your mind.

Your mindset is the manifestation of your thoughts—essentially, what you believe. However, it's your Mindwomb that governs the conditions that feed your mind, influencing how we shape these beliefs. It's about how we nurture our thoughts and ideas, demonstrating our considerable power over the results that materialize in our lives. The Bible, in Colossians 3:2 (AMP), inspires us to "set your mind *and* keep it focused *habitually* on the things above [the heavenly things], not on things that are on the earth [which have only temporal value]." The scripture provides explicit instruction that emphasizes the importance of intentional thinking, directing us to focus on the "things above"— the promises of God. We hold the power to choose what nourishes our minds. The food for our thoughts is drawn from our senses—what we see, taste, touch, smell, and feel. This sensory input substantially influences the outcomes that unfold in our lives. Therefore, the deliberate and mindful nurturing of your Mindwomb requires the consistent and constant direction of your thoughts. It's this level of effort that lays the foundation that's receptive to personal growth and change, enabling you to evolve into your best self and live life on your own terms.

The nurturing of your Mindwomb also serves as a potent acknowledgment of your worth as a creation of God. This acknowledgment is not just about self-affirmation but a recognition of God's divine love for you. In understanding your worthiness, you grasp that you are deserving of God's love. This profound love was demonstrated when He sacrificed His only Son for our salvation. As stated in John 3:16 (NIV), "For God so loved the world that he gave his one and only Son, that whoever believes in him shall not perish but have eternal life." This is the measure of your worthiness in the eyes of God—a worthiness that permits you to live an abundant life. In caring for your Mindwomb, you cultivate this understanding, affirming your value and opening the way to live life as God intended for you.

THE JOURNEY FROM CULTURAL CONDITIONING

I lost my mother at the tender age of five, and my father, who appeared in my life only briefly during my adult years, was frequently absent due to intermittent incarceration. Consequently, I was brought up in a single-grandparent household, which created a significant generational gap of over half a century between us. My grandmother's life unfolded against the backdrop of some of the most tumultuous periods in American history. Born in the era of the Great Depression, her formative years were scarred by the strife of World War II and the aftermath. She lived through the peak of segregation, the oppressive chains of Jim Crow laws, and the enduring menace of racial violence. The Civil Rights Movement of the 1950s and 1960s, a period of profound change and turbulence, imprinted deeply on her consciousness.

Her adult years witnessed pivotal moments of transformation: the Brown vs. Board of Education decision in 1954, the Civil Rights Act of 1964, and the Voting Rights Act of 1965. Yet, these monumental legal victories couldn't fully eradicate the pervasive systemic racism, economic disparities, and the lingering remnants of segregation that she continued to experience. By the time I was born, she faced the harsh realities of her existence every day, dealing with constant struggles and inequality. These circumstances led to continuous clashes in our home. Growing up, I found the differences in our life experiences, values, and general perspectives on life hard to reconcile. Often, I felt judged and misunderstood. But, with the clarity of hindsight, I can see that our disagreements stemmed from good intentions that had strayed off course. While my grandmother intended to be the best parent, she was misguided by believing the best way of parenting me was based on her experiences, goals, and needs, rather than being open to understanding mine.

My grandmother always emphasized the necessity for me to maintain a deep sense of gratitude for any opportunities that came my way. Her insistence was firmly anchored in her historical awareness, a time when Black individuals were denied the right to share the same spaces as white people. Therefore, I was taught to appreciate every opportunity, irrespective of whether these opportunities were coupled with unfair wages or inequitable conditions. For example, the concept of negotiating a job offer was a conversation never held and a concept I'd never heard of—the focus was simply on being grateful for the offer and opportunity.

In retrospect, I recognize that I shortchanged myself in my first job offer, accepting a salary almost $15,000 dollars less than my colleague, not because the company was unfair but simply because my colleague asked for it, and I didn't. My Mindwomb was starved of the necessary nutrients that would inspire me to question, negotiate, or expect more. It had been nurtured to believe that asking for more was synonymous with ingratitude, and that would ultimately jeopardize the opportunity itself. To my grandmother, despite the systemic inequalities, discrimination, and racism that persist today, she regarded my very consideration for the job as a mark of privilege. For her, the offer alone was an achievement to be celebrated, a success she herself had never enjoyed.

I was raised in a world where barred windows and locked chain-link fences were standard, where corner stores were our regular snack hubs, and metro buses served as transportation to more distant locations. This was my world, and in my grandmother's eyes, it was a good life. My Mindwomb fed this limited belief—I didn't need to strive for more because, in my mind, we were already living well, or so I thought. My grandmother operated in a survivalist mindset, which created a generational perspective that often clashed with my own, but I now understand better the historical and cultural forces that shaped her, and how it was those same cultural forces that raised me.

◇◇◇◇◇◇◇◇◇◇◇◇◇◇◇◇◇◇◇◇◇◇◇◇◇◇◇◇◇◇◇◇

As I embarked on my journey of self-discovery, I started a profound transformative process that entailed reprogramming my mind to perceive my worth and power from an entirely new perspective.

As I embarked on my journey of self-discovery, I started a profound transformative process that entailed reprogramming my mind to perceive my worth and power from an entirely new perspective. I came to the realization that the reins to my life are firmly held in my hands; the choices I make, the experiences I invite into my life, and the path my life journey takes all stem from me. I had to recondition my mind to truly grasp this. In essence, mastering your mindset is about taking control of your inner narrative, rewriting your story from a place of strength and potential, and ultimately, leading a life that is not just lived but equally owned and cherished.

My voyage of self-discovery led to the shattering of ingrained cultural conditionings that lived subconsciously within me. It prompted a pivot in my perspective, propelling me to nurture and broaden my Mindwomb. This journey made it clear that there was a pressing need to reeducate myself, to unlearn certain preconceived notions, and to release the limiting beliefs that were restricting my faith from imagining outcomes beyond the anticipated. I came to understand that if a thought can find space in my mind, God possesses the ability to exceed it. So, why limit myself to my humble comprehension when it stands no match to the boundless potential that God embodies?

The Bible affirms this in Ephesians 3:20 (AMP), promising us that God can perform far beyond our prayers, hopes, or dreams:

Now to Him who is able to [carry out His purpose and] do
superabundantly more than all that we dare ask or think
[infinitely beyond our greatest prayers, hopes, or dreams],
according to His power that is at work within us.

This knowledge reinforces the idea that if a notion can be conceived within my mind, there must be something of even grander magnitude waiting. I am resolved not to miss my moment of receiving all that God has designated for me.

THE SELFLESS ACT OF SELF-MASTERY

Self-mastery, in this context, is an empowering journey of intentional transformation. It is the conscious, continuous effort to channel your thoughts in a direction that resonates with your potential and aligns with the brighter destiny that awaits you. Rather than succumbing to the thought patterns that have been ingrained in us through our upbringing or circumstances, self-mastery teaches us to assert control over our thought processes.

By achieving self-mastery, you gain the power to let go of beliefs, habits, or traits that no longer serve you and impede your journey toward your highest potential. This involves a process of insightful course correction, identifying areas that need change, and substituting them with more positive, constructive patterns of thought and behavior. This metamorphic journey turns you into the architect of your own life, granting you the authority to design your destiny, brick by brick, thought by thought. You don't just live life as it comes, but rather, you construct your life to live as you envision it.

Self-mastery brings about a profound realization and appreciation of your value. You, as an individual, are a sacred space, a dwelling place of God. This is emphasized in 1 Corinthians 3:16 (CEV), which states, "All of you surely know you are God's temple and his Spirit lives in you." So, the journey to self-mastery begins with investing time in introspection, thereby creating space for communion with God. God desires to reveal to you the aspects of yourself that remain hidden. You cannot fully comprehend your limitless potential, nor can you continuously grow, learn, and evolve without focusing on the various dimensions of "self." By consciously prioritizing these dimensions, you inadvertently prioritize your mental well-being.

When I started this journey, I dedicated one hour each day, consistently at the same time, to focus on myself. There were no distractions and no cell phones. My family was aware that this was my "Do Not Disturb" period; it was my "me time." I would comfortably position myself in my personal space, with my journal and pen in hand, ready to receive what God had to communicate to me. It wasn't a moment for a two-way conversation of prayer; it was intentional time for me to sit in silence and listen. We often overlook that prayer is communication with God, yet once we've voiced our requests, we sometimes forget to pause and listen for His guidance or response.

During these precious moments, I embarked on honing my self-mastery skills, methodically examining their diverse aspects. Each component was noted down, with me scrutinizing and determining the necessary steps to be taken if needed. I focused on the following self-mastery areas:

◊ Self-love, which involves embracing your uniqueness and acknowledging your inherent worth.
◊ Self-care, which entails taking care of your physical, mental, and emotional health.

◇ Self-acceptance, which means embracing imperfections without feeling the need to change.
◇ Self-fulfillment, which relates to the realization of your personal desires and aspirations.
◇ Self-actualization, which is the ongoing journey of realizing and fulfilling your potential.
◇ Self-knowledge, which implies a deep understanding of your personality, including your strengths, weaknesses, thoughts, beliefs, motivations, and emotions.
◇ Self-approval, which means recognizing your worth and being proud of your accomplishments.
◇ Self-promotion, which involves presenting yourself effectively and accurately.
◇ Self-discipline, which relates to your ability to control your feelings and overcome your weaknesses.
◇ Self-worth, which is your understanding of your value and worthiness.

Fundamental to this philosophy is the recognition that the worth you assign to yourself significantly influences your self-treatment. Simply put, how you view yourself shapes your decisions, your actions, and ultimately, your destiny.

◇◇◇◇◇◇◇◇◇◇◇◇◇◇◇◇◇◇◇◇◇◇◇◇◇◇◇◇◇◇◇◇

Simply put, how you view yourself shapes your decisions, your actions, and ultimately, your destiny.

BE GRATEFUL FOR REJECTION

Rewinding a few years, I found myself engrossed in an interview for an enticing HR role at Wayfair, a renowned furniture manufacturing and distribution company. I was excited with anticipation; every detail of the job description seemed to align with my expertise and aspirations. After navigating through two rounds of interviews, I felt an undeniable certainty that I had left a solid impression. Then came an unforeseen phone call from the hiring manager. He labeled my interview as "unexpected." *Unexpected?* my mind repeated. He went on to reveal that although my interaction with him had been refreshingly enjoyable, the decision had been made to move forward with an internal candidate.

A wave of disbelief washed over me. The sting of rejection pierced through my confidence, leaving me crushed and disheartened. The words of approval from the interview rounds now seemed hollow, swelling my embarrassment. I couldn't understand why or how this was happening, especially after intensely praying for this opportunity. Adding to my confusion was the fact that I was approached for this role; I did not even actively pursue it! This detail had reinforced my belief that this opportunity had to be God-led. How, then, could it all culminate in such a gut-wrenching response? And then, this happened—roughly three months following that turn-down conversation, a startling headline blared from the newspaper: "Wayfair layoffs impact 580 employees." My heart pounded as I read on, with a scrolling journey through LinkedIn only intensifying my shock. The job cuts had sliced through the HR department.

Looking back, I can't help but think I truly dodged a bullet! At first, the sting of rejection had me questioning God's plans for me. But rather than dwell on the "whys" or reach out to the recruiter in frustration, I chose to lean into my faith. I trusted that this setback was a part of His bigger plan for me. Holding onto that faith, especially when it seemed in conflict with what was happening, wasn't easy. Yet, the reward of this faith was undeniable. By not getting that role, I was saved from a position that would've left me jobless in just a few months' time.

Traditionally, people define rejection as receiving a negative response to a heartfelt desire. When it's something you've really wanted or hoped for, that "no" can be shattering. But what if what you were wanting or hoping for wasn't in alignment with God's plan for your life? Would you still want it? Jeremiah 29:11 (AMP) tells us, "For I know the plans *and* thoughts that I have for you,' says the LORD, 'plans for peace *and* well-being and not for disaster, to give you a future and a hope."

◇◇◇◇◇◇◇◇◇◇◇◇◇◇◇◇◇◇◇◇◇◇◇◇◇◇◇◇◇◇◇◇◇◇◇◇

To me, rejection is a non-existent concept;
it simply signifies that something grander
and more fitting is on the horizon for me.

You see, the rejection was not a setback; rather, it was a stepping stone. We worship a God who possesses vision beyond our sight. And in my reformed mindset, I had to undergo the process of mental reprogramming. If you ask me about rejection now, my response will be that to me, rejection is a non-existent concept; it simply signifies that something grander and more fitting is on the horizon for me. After this revelation, and realizing I avoided what would have been an unfortunate situation, I thanked God for loving me enough to allow me to get the "no" that kept me employed.

As stated in 2 Corinthians 4:8-9, we are vessels filled with immense power with a treasure from the Lord. We have the power and authority to construct a belief system that will fulfill our requests and demands. This scripture explicitly reminds us:

> We often suffer, but we are never crushed. Even when we don't know what to do, we never give up. In times of trouble, God is with us, and when we are knocked down, we get up again. (CEV)

With such divine assurance, how can we allow denial to intimidate us?

EMBRACING YOUR DIVINE WORTH

Recognizing your true worth allows your mind to see only greatness, especially when you align with your divine purpose. Remember, you are destined for more than you can imagine. God crafted you with plans for abundance, leadership, and peace. Understand that challenges are momentary, just passing seasons. Every storm fades, and with each new day comes joy. If ever in doubt, firmly hold onto the belief that greater blessings await because you deserve nothing less. There may be moments when you question this truth, but it is during these times you must cling to what you know to be absolute. This is because your mind is a powerful manifestor—what you lead it to believe, it will create. Embrace the mindset of abundance, prosperity, and greatness, and that will be your reality.

DISMANTLING MINDSET BARRIERS

Now is the time to confront and unmask those deeply ingrained beliefs that have held you back, acting as silent inhibitors to your progress. Think of them as invisible walls that you've unknowingly built over time. One of the most profound barriers I personally dealt with was an intense fear of rejection. But through deliberate reflection and mindset work, I've reshaped my thinking, refusing to be governed by the paralyzing grip of denial.

It's vital to understand that our mental barriers, often, are self-imposed. They're the culmination of past experiences, societal and cultural conditioning, and negative internal dialogues. While these barriers might feel real and tangible, with dedicated effort, they can be deconstructed.

Embarking on the transformative journey to recalibrate your mindset isn't just about identifying barriers; it's about actively integrating practices that foster growth and resilience. Here are some pivotal strategies that have been instrumental in my own journey:

◇ Daily Affirmations: Kickstart each day with a series of positive affirmations. This simple yet powerful ritual not only sets an optimistic tone but, over time, gradually changes your mindset.

◇ Mindful Reflection: Pay attention to your present situation without judgment. This practice helps you accept your current situation and reduces the likelihood of negative thought patterns.

◇ Cultivate Gratitude: Shifting the lens from scarcity to abundance, regular gratitude practices can alter your focus from what's missing to the plethora of blessings already in your life.

◇ Commit to Continuous Learning: Dive into books and materials that challenge and inspire. By continuously expanding your knowledge, you're inherently broadening your horizons and understanding.

◊ Mind Your Circle: Remember, energy is contagious. Surrounding yourself with individuals who lift, inspire, and motivate can play a pivotal role in shaping your mindset.

◊ Prioritize Self: Above all, make yourself a priority. When you invest time in nurturing your well-being and understanding your essence, it provides clarity, purpose, and an enriched perspective on life's events.

By adopting these practices, you're assured of a mental restructuring that firmly supports the belief that even the seemingly adverse situations are working out for your favor.

chapter 6

INFLUENCE: YOUR GREATNESS IS ROOTED IN A BELIEF AND VALUE SYSTEM

To reach the Pinnacle of Greatness, we must be unwavering and succinct in aligning actions with deeply held beliefs and values. This isn't only about personal coherence; it's a spiritual imperative. When our actions resonate clearly with our convictions, it creates a pathway for God to position us optimally in His grand design. Just as a master craftsman needs the right tool in the right place for his masterpiece, God, too, seeks to place us precisely where our strengths, molded by our beliefs and values, can be most impactful.

By being steadfast in this alignment, we not only bolster our personal journey as Greatness but also allow God to leverage our unique gifts and talents to fulfill a divine purpose that is far grander than any we could conceive on our own. To fulfill God's vision for our lives, it's vital to clearly understand our values and core beliefs, knowing what they are foundationally based upon and how they influence our decisions. With this awareness, not only do we achieve a profound understanding of ourselves, but we also make choices that consistently align with the image we embrand to the world.

CORE BELIEFS AND VALUES—WHAT ARE THEY?

Core beliefs are the fundamental convictions or principles we hold, often stemming from upbringing, experiences, culture, and personal reflections. They shape our worldview and our understanding of ourselves and the universe. For instance, I might have a core belief that "the world is a dangerous place," or "I am worthy of love and respect." Core beliefs can be positive or limiting and generally operate at a deep, often subconscious, level.

Your values, on the other hand, are the ideals and standards you use as a guide for your behaviors and decisions. They help determine what is important, right, or desirable. They are as unique as your fingerprint, representing your innermost beliefs and fueling your actions. Think of them as your personal GPS, directing your decisions and experiences that align with who you are deep down. Values also help us decide how we spend our time, whom we associate with, and how we approach challenges.

Think of core beliefs as the roots of a tree. They are foundational, offering support and feeding the tree's growth. They act as the primary lens through which we perceive the world, whether we're aware of them or not. Values, on the other hand, are like the fruits or leaves of the tree. They are the tangible manifestations of our core beliefs—visible, explicit expressions sharing who we are and what's important to us. Just as the health of a tree's roots can impact the quality of its fruits, our core beliefs significantly influence what we value. For example, let's say a person has an underlying belief that every individual has worth. This might lead them to hold the values of inclusivity and fairness. Their belief about human worth directly translates to their value system, pushing them to advocate for equal rights and opportunities for everyone.

Overall, core beliefs are the deeply held truths that shape our worldview, and values are the guiding principles derived from these beliefs. Together, they form a belief system that influences every facet of our lives, from daily decisions to long-term goals. Both play essential roles in our behaviors, shaping our perceptions and influencing our life choices. Ensuring harmony between your core beliefs and values is crucial. When they're in alignment, it fosters a sense of coherence and authenticity in life. However, conflicts arise when our values-driven actions contradict our deeper beliefs.

◇◇◇◇◇◇◇◇◇◇◇◇◇◇◇◇◇◇◇◇◇◇◇◇◇◇◇◇◇◇◇◇◇◇◇◇

Overall, core beliefs are the deeply held truths that shape our worldview, and values are the guiding principles derived from these beliefs.

THE IMPACT OF MISALIGNMENT ON REPUTATION

When our actions don't align with the values we publicly endorse and embrand, it becomes a question of integrity and authenticity in the eyes of others; it can significantly impact our reputation. As an example, if I claim to support startup entrepreneurs but charge steep prices for my services, believing my expertise justifies doing so, then one might question whether nurturing the next wave of business owners is truly a foundational belief of mine. Advocating to value helping new business startups while simultaneously setting high, exorbitant fees, making it challenging for a budding entrepreneur to afford, raises eyebrows, and it can create distaste in the public.

The disconnect between charging high prices and the stated value creates an inconsistency that can lead people to question your authenticity. People may start to wonder, *Do you genuinely care about uplifting young entrepreneurs, or is it just a marketing tactic?* When individuals or businesses display a misalignment between what they say and what they do, it tarnishes their reputation. They might be labeled as inauthentic, untrustworthy, or even opportunistic. These doubts can lead to skepticism and erode the trust that others place in you.

Over time, this skepticism can overshadow your positive contributions, no matter how significant they might be. In a world that holds authenticity in high regard, ensuring our actions consistently mirror our values and beliefs is essential. When these seem contradictory, it sows doubt and suspicion. It's not just about one action being questioned; it's about our overall credibility being scrutinized.

THE IMPACT OF MISALIGNMENT ON CREDIBILITY

Consistency between our beliefs, values, and actions is also crucial for maintaining the credibility of not just ourselves but also who or what we say we represent. When people sense inconsistency, they may feel misled or think that you're not truly representing who you say you are or what you say you believe. In the long run, this perception can deter potential collaborations, partnerships, or clients who value genuineness.

Recently, as I organized the UNPLUG HR Conference, I sought speakers exemplifying the essence of our theme which was centered on being who you were created to be, unapologetically. The idea was to spotlight those who had genuinely maintained their identity, even if it meant turning down lucrative opportunities. A renowned entrepreneur stood out for her resolute commitment to authenticity, even when a major media outlet offered her vast exposure in exchange for altering her tone, appearance, and image. My team sent out a proposal, and I was thrilled when we received a response expressing interest in exploring a potential collaboration.

Shortly after, my excitement took a backseat when her team quoted a fee of $150k for an hour, not including first-class travel for her and her team. While I anticipated covering a speaker's fee, travel, and accommodations, I hadn't expected a sum that could practically purchase a home for just an hour of her time to discuss something she portrayed in her brand—to be a champion of authenticity. The high fee also seemed incongruous with her public persona, particularly her advocacy for supporting fellow Black businesses. The experience left me questioning the alignment between her projected values and the underlying beliefs guiding her brand.

◇◇◇◇◇◇◇◇◇◇◇◇◇◇◇◇◇◇◇◇◇◇◇◇◇◇◇◇◇◇◇◇◇◇

Your personal representation of what you stand for should be consistently reflected by those speaking or acting on your behalf, even in your absence.

My team shared my disbelief, speculating that perhaps she was unaware of how her team conducted business on her behalf. This brings me to a brief yet essential point I'd like to emphasize: those who serve as the face for your brand—your team, employees, or any representatives—must align with your values and beliefs. Your personal representation of what you stand for should be consistently reflected by those speaking or acting on your behalf, even in your absence. These are things you should be uncovering when conducting your job interviews and screening process when expanding your team. Public interactions involving anyone associated with your brand should be seamless to the point where if an email were sent without a signature, they shouldn't be able to discern whether it was from you or a team member. This level of synergy is vital not only for cohesive brand representation but also for your credibility.

Ultimately, I did reach out to the entrepreneur I was looking to book, seeking clarity on the situation, but I haven't received a response yet. I'd like to believe she's unaware of the representation of her brand. This is why I'm refraining from revealing her identity now as I aim to discuss this with her directly before drawing any conclusions. I share this as an example to underscore how imperative it is to ensure actions and branding genuinely mirror professed beliefs and values. When there's a misalignment between our stated values and beliefs, evidenced by our actions, it can significantly impact our credibility. Recognizing and addressing any dissonance between the two paves the way for a more fulfilling and purposeful life.

THE IMPACT OF MISALIGNMENT IN RELATIONSHIPS

In every interaction, every partnership, and every transaction, there's an underlying agreement—a silent affirmation that the values held by both parties are, to some extent, aligned. When we choose to engage with someone, be it personally or professionally, we're sending a message. We're stating, even if it's subconsciously, "I see a reflection of my values in you." When you're firm in your values, you naturally draw toward circumstances and people that reflect them. This creates an environment rich in mutual respect, understanding, and genuine connections.

Ensuring an alignment in values and beliefs among the company you keep isn't just preferable, it's essential. As humans, when our core beliefs misalign with others, it invariably sets the stage for ongoing disputes. Collaborative efforts then become a minefield of misunderstandings, justifying behaviors, and defending viewpoints, an overall disruption of the harmonious flow in the relationship. This principle isn't new; the Bible reinforces this concept of alignment in Amos 3:3 (NKJV): "Can two walk together, unless they are agreed?" This isn't merely a rhetorical question—it's a profound insight into human relationships. The premise of this scripture is clear: for any significant partnership or journey, there must be a foundational agreement in core beliefs, values, or vision.

Sometimes, people find themselves drained and disillusioned in their professional relationships, friendships, and partnerships, often feeling trapped in a cycle of endless bickering and conflict. Generally, the root of these struggles lies in a deep-seated misalignment of core beliefs or values. This is more than just clashing personalities—it's about having fundamentally different perspectives and priorities.

Second Corinthians 6:14 (AMP) urges:

Do not be unequally bound together with unbelievers [do not make mismatched alliances with them, inconsistent with your faith]. For what partnership can righteousness have with lawlessness? Or what fellowship can light have with darkness?

This scripture prompts us to reflect deeply: As a believer, what shared purpose can you genuinely have with an unbeliever? What genuine connection can we foster with someone who doesn't share our belief system? The phrase "unequally yoked" implies that there's a lack of mutual understanding, which is a recipe for conflict and inefficiency.

The Message translation of 2 Corinthians 6:14 leaves little room for ambiguity about the consequences of relationship misalignment. It asks rhetorically:

How can you make a partnership out of right and wrong? That's not partnership; that's war. Is light best friends with dark? Does Christ go strolling with the Devil? Do trust and mistrust hold hands?"

These provocative questions underscore the friction and tension that emerge when conflicting belief systems meet.

The scriptural implications are clear: when there are vast inconsistencies in values and belief systems, forming a symbiotic relationship, hoping to yield meaningful results, is nonsensical and counterproductive. With such a profound difference in our core beliefs, the foundation for mutual understanding and agreement would be ineffective at best, leading to missed opportunities for both parties. So, ensuring alignment is not just beneficial; it's also scriptural.

Anything that you engage in that does not align with your values will naturally feel incongruent, as though you are compromising a fundamental part of yourself. Compromise, in this context, implies bending or overlooking your values just to adapt or conform to a specific situation or individual. If you're uncertain or not firmly grounded in your core beliefs, you can easily find yourself manipulated. This lack of clarity can lead you into behaviors, situations, or relationships that are fundamentally misaligned with who you are. The result? Discomfort, dissatisfaction, and potentially, a sense of lost identity. So, having a strong understanding and commitment to your values is paramount in living a fulfilling and authentic life.

◇◇◇◇◇◇◇◇◇◇◇◇◇◇◇◇◇◇◇◇◇◇◇◇◇◇◇◇◇◇◇◇◇

If you're uncertain or not firmly grounded in your core beliefs, you can easily find yourself manipulated.

THE UNSPOKEN POWER OF VALUES

While many of us might claim that we operate within a set of values, few have made the deliberate effort to articulate and understand them fully. Have you ever paused to reflect on the beliefs and values that shape your life? I'm not talking about the generalized principles society often mentions, like honesty or kindness but the deeply personal convictions that resonate within you—values and beliefs that, when compromised, leave you feeling unsettled. Take a moment now. List your core beliefs and the values that branch from them. Now, are those results a reflection of how you behave? Do others see these values in action when they interact with you? This isn't just an exercise; it's an invitation to discover what core beliefs drive your every action. Recognizing and embracing these facets are paramount in leading a life of alignment and fulfillment, especially as a representative of Christ.

Even corporations recognize the power of values. As a part of most branding strategies, companies place significant importance on defining their values. It's evident in the way they deliberately highlight their core principles, not tucked away in a corner but blasted front and center for all to see. Look around, and you'll notice that successful businesses have long understood the magnetic pull of creating shared values. Their values are posted on websites, in office spaces, and through advertising campaigns. It's a statement, a promise, a badge of honor they wear to tell the world, "This is who we are."

They do this because they understand values aren't just words on paper; they are powerful marketing tools and foundational pillars. Values operate as unseen forces that subtly influence choices, nudging us in directions that best resonate with our beliefs. It's how they attract consumers who they know will be interested in what they offer. Consider, for instance, an environmentally conscious person who prioritizes eco-friendly products. When they come across a brand emphasizing its commitment to sustainability, recycling, and reducing its carbon footprint, they feel an immediate connection. The brand isn't just selling a product; it's selling an idea, a belief, a value system. It's as if the brand is speaking directly to their heart, resonating with who they are.

In that same respect, your personal values aren't just silent beliefs tucked away inside your heart; they loudly proclaim who you are through your actions, decisions, and behaviors. If you deeply value honesty, your friends might not even consider asking you to cover for them in a lie. They already know your answer without even posing the question. It's as if you wear your values, not as badges on your chest but as an impression that surrounds you.

◇◇◇◇◇◇◇◇◇◇◇◇◇◇◇◇◇◇◇◇◇◇◇◇◇◇◇◇◇◇◇◇

Your personal values aren't just silent beliefs tucked away inside your heart; they loudly proclaim who you are through your actions, decisions, and behaviors.

Think about this: How often have people anticipated your responses or decisions based on the principles they've seen you uphold time and again? What behaviors or situations do your loved ones know, without a doubt, you'd never engage in? This silent understanding, this unspoken recognition, speaks volumes about how powerfully your values are received. So, take a moment for introspection: What do people see in you? What unspoken messages are you sending through your choices, demeanor, and boundaries? Remember, you might not always voice your values explicitly, but they do become evident in the way you live.

DID YOU LIST LOVE?

For those who profess to be believers, love should stand as an obvious core belief and a lived value. It's the foundational cornerstone of our faith. Valuing a lifestyle reflective of Christ is not just about outwardly showing love—it's about prioritizing love; it's about genuinely being it. The Bible is clear in its directive about love. John 13:34 (AMP) says, "I am giving you a new commandment, that you love one another. Just as I have loved you, so you too are to love on another."

DON'T JUST SHOW LOVE—BE LOVE

Traditionally, many believers interpret God's command to love as an urge to "show" love. However, there's a fundamental difference between "showing" love and "being" love. When we *show* love, it's often conditional—it can be turned on or off depending on the circumstance or the person in question. But to *be* love is to have it ingrained in us unconditionally. Changing behaviors, or simply showing love, is temporary and selective. But being love, in its truest form, becomes a part of our very character, consistent in our interactions with others.

Every one of us has love infused into our DNA—it's a core part of who we are, and who we were created to be. The challenge arises when individuals choose to express love selectively, offering it based on convenience or preference. These selective displays aren't in alignment with God's instructions. He calls us to "be" love, in every situation, to every person, reflecting His own boundless and overwhelming love.

To truly follow Jesus means we don't simply display love, but we fully embody it. When people meet us, they shouldn't just witness acts of love; they should consistently experience genuine love through our actions and exchanges. Turning to 1 Corinthians 13, we see a clear outline of love defined: it's patient and kind, not envious, jealous, boastful, or proud. Love doesn't dishonor others, is not self-seeking, is not easily angered, and keeps no record of wrongs (holding grudges). Love rejoices in the truth and always protects, trusts, hopes, and perseveres. Using this as a yardstick, measure your behavior. Are you steadfast in being love? Are these attributes evident in your life? If there's a discrepancy, then the hard question surfaces: are you inadvertently misrepresenting the God you profess to serve and follow?

LIVE LIFE WITH LOVE AS A CORE BELIEF

When love is a core belief, it manifests as more than a feeling—it becomes the foundation from which all values are expressed. A person rooted in love will naturally exude compassion, which compels them to empathize with others and act selflessly. Kindness flows from them effortlessly, making every interaction a gentle touch. Patience becomes a quiet strength, allowing them to endure and support others through their struggles without judgment.

Living with love as a core belief is also characterized by a quiet but profound strength—forgiveness. You will understand human frailty and choose to offer second chances, mirroring the grace you yourself have also received. Your integrity ensures that your words and actions align, making you trustworthy and transparent. Your generosity, both in spirit and in deed, reflects your understanding that love is about giving, sometimes sacrificially. Faithfulness to commitments and to people is a natural outcome, cultivating deep bonds and trust. These values, when lived genuinely, not only will define your character but also become a silent testimony of your love for God as His creation. You don't just speak about love; you'll exemplify it in every facet of your life.

Imagine this fictitious story of Minister Kate, a respected figure in her church community. Many members of her congregation turn to her for spiritual guidance and wisdom. However, outside the church's sanctuary, Kate's actions tell a different story. She often shares content on social media that seems out of place for a spiritual leader. In her professional life, where she's a manager, her subordinates frequently feel undercut by her words and actions. They describe her as unapproachable, seemingly bitter, and angry.

Now, envision someone unfamiliar with Christianity who works with Kate. For them, Kate's behavior could become their reference for what Christianity stands for. They might wonder, *Is this what faith promotes?* This raises a crucial question for all believers: are our actions drawing people closer to understanding God's love or pushing them away? When love is a core belief you embrace, others will see in you a resilience that makes them wonder, *How can she maintain her peace during such adversity?* or *Why would he lend a hand to someone who wronged him?* Living as love means mirroring God's love in every situation. This is why love must be an emphasized value in our belief system.

Living as God, who is the epitome of love, intends for us to live requires obedience. The blessings and guarantees He offers are tied to our commitment to His principles. And the Bible is quite clear in John 15:17 (AMP), "This [is what] I command you: that you love and unselfishly seek the best for one another." If we overlook or ignore His instructions, can we genuinely expect to receive His blessings, especially when we want them on our timetable? Embracing love's characteristics, both in speech and in action, is key to following the path God has paved for us to live as His design. Only then, can we aim to experience His full blessings.

If we declare our life in Christ, there's a fundamental responsibility that accompanies this profession. First John 2:6 challenges us to walk just as Christ did, with love at the forefront of our conduct:

Whoever says he lives in Christ [that is, whoever says he has accepted Him as God's Son] ought to walk and conduct himself just as He walked and conducted Himself.

This isn't about exhibiting love; it's about ensuring that love, along with kindness, patience, and the other fruits of the spirit, is ingrained in our identity. As we aspire toward the Pinnacle of Greatness, it's paramount that these values not only be displayed but truly lived. By embodying these Christlike virtues, we inch closer to fulfilling God's design for us, influencing others to draw near to Him and reap the true rewards of a faith-led life.

THE PATHWAY TO LIVING AS GREATNESS

Our journey in this life is an intricate shuffle of beliefs, values, and actions, but the beauty of this dance is not in perfection; it's in the consistent effort to align with the divine rhythm established by our Creator. Every step and every decision are opportunities to express our Greatness as our distinguished identity, reflecting the image of God within us. Embracing this identity means resisting the pull to conform to the world's fleeting standards, instead choosing to uphold the eternal values entrusted to us. By doing so, we move closer to the purpose God has for us—radiating His light, His love, and His truth— igniting the highest levels of our greatness. It's in this alignment, in the symphony of our beliefs resonating with our *actions*, that we find ourselves grounded firmly in divine purpose.

◇◇◇◇◇◇◇◇◇◇◇◇◇◇◇◇◇◇◇◇◇◇◇◇◇◇◇◇◇◇◇◇◇

Our journey in this life is an intricate shuffle of beliefs, values, and actions, but the beauty of this dance is not in perfection; it's in the consistent effort to align with the divine rhythm established by our Creator.

Allow this prayer to serve as a source of inspiration and solace as you strive for alignment of your values and beliefs:

A PRAYER FOR AUTHENTIC ALIGNMENT

Dear Heavenly Father,

In every breath and step I take, let Your great commandment—to love as Christ loves us—be the compass that guides me. In moments of doubt, anchor me in the truths You've placed in my heart.

Help me to not only show love but to become an embodiment of Your love in my daily interactions, reflecting the sacrificial love of Jesus. Help me represent the values You've given with unwavering strength, and when the world suggests I conform, remind me of Your unique design for my life.

Grant me the courage to live out the values You cherish, resisting the call to blend in with the world, but instead, shining with the distinctive light You've given me. Let Your Spirit dwell richly within me, that every action and word I extend to others may be a testament to the love that flows from You. Let Your Spirit guide my steps, affirming my true identity in You. In Your name. Amen.

chapter 7

CONTRIBUTION: YOUR GREATNESS PRESCRIBES A VALUABLE OFFERING

In the preceding chapter, we discussed the integral role our values system plays in our lives. These are the pillars that uphold our moral compass, steering our choices, and refining our decision-making. These core values become the touchstones of our character, helping us navigate the complexities of right and wrong. However, there is another dimension of value that extends beyond the internal landscape of our ethics. This is the individual value we bring to the table—the spectrum of our talents, insights, expertise, and life lessons that we share in our social and professional circles. For clarity, we will refer to these individual values that are external manifestations of our inner principles as our "Value Offerings."

In the vast expanse of human life, two primary elements characterize us: our foundational beliefs (that nourish the core values we cherish) and the unique Value Offerings that arise from our individual identities. Though they may seem separate at first glance, they are inextricably linked, shaping our identity to dictate the course of our life's journey. To better understand this, let's revisit the tree analogy from the previous chapter.

Do you remember our analogy where we associated core beliefs to be like the roots of a tree? Deeply implanted, they provide the foundation that gives life to the entire structure. They are pivotal, offering support, nourishment, and dictating the overall health of the tree. These beliefs, often hidden beneath the surface, determine the quality and essence of what the tree can offer. Core values, then, are the branches and leaves of this tree—extensions and expressions of these deep-seated beliefs. They wave in the wind, interact with the world, and create the identity of the tree, illustrating to everyone what the tree stands for and believes in.

Now, consider the tree's fruits as your Value Offering. These fruits are what the world tangibly receives and benefits from. They're the direct result of healthy roots (core beliefs) and strong branches (core values). When someone comes into your shade, they're not just looking for momentary relief; they're hoping to taste the unique fruits you offer. This is the experience, wisdom, and influence you share with others. It's the practical, tangible impact of your existence on those around you. Just as the health of the roots and branches determines the quality of the fruit, the authenticity and depth of your core beliefs and values shape the richness and impact of your Value Offering to the world.

◇◇◇◇◇◇◇◇◇◇◇◇◇◇◇◇◇◇◇◇◇◇◇◇◇◇◇◇◇◇◇◇

When someone comes into your shade, they're not just looking for a momentary relief; they're hoping to taste the unique fruits you offer.

FROM CORE VALUES TO LASTING IMPACT

Our core values have a great influence on our Value Offerings. The unique value we bring to the world is the lasting impression left on everyone we meet, the comfort we provide, the problems we solve, and the imprint we leave in our service. For example, if honesty ranks high as a core value, it naturally leads us to foster trust and reliability in all our dealings. Similarly, if we highly regard creativity as a core value, our Value Offering might manifest as revolutionary ideas or novel approaches to challenges. Value Offerings answer crucial needs and address pivotal concerns for others. They're embedded in your identity, the unique blend of qualities you possess, designed to serve and enrich others' lives. A true measure of your significance is found in the positive impact you create in others' lives through the value you contribute.

The beauty of understanding our core values and their influence on our Value Offerings is that it allows us to serve with purpose and integrity. It's not just about what we do but the intention and heart behind it. As we navigate our daily lives, let's be conscious of the lasting footprints we leave in the sands of time. Every interaction, no matter how small, holds the potential to be a testament to our values and the unique gifts we offer to the world. In the end, our legacy is not just about what we've achieved for ourselves but also about what we've contributed to others. It is the remnants of our actions, the residue of our authenticity, and the evidence of our commitment to our core values. As you reflect upon your own life, consider the trail of contribution you've left behind. Does it speak to the diversity of your gifts, recognizing the value only you can offer?

Remember, the impact of a single life is immeasurable. Your Value Offerings, whether they are moments of kindness, innovative solutions, or a dedication to excellence, ripple out into the world in ways you might never fully comprehend. So, embrace your core values. Let them steer you toward making contributions that not only fill a need but also fulfill a higher purpose. As you do so, you become a living testament to the power of aligning what is most important to you with what you give back to the world. So again, embrace your values, recognize the worth you bring, and take pride in knowing that, in your own special way, you are making the world a better place for others.

◇◇◇◇◇◇◇◇◇◇◇◇◇◇◇◇◇◇◇◇◇◇◇◇◇◇◇◇◇◇◇◇

This is the essence of greatness—when what we value and what we offer converge to create something truly meaningful and lasting.

This is the essence of greatness—when what we value and what we offer converge to create something truly meaningful and lasting. Strive to leave a legacy that resonates with your core values, and watch as your Value Offerings become your mark of distinction in a world that needs the richness of your genuine contributions.

ADDRESSING THE WHITE SPACE: DIFFERENTIATING YOUR VALUE OFFERING

In a world filled with noise and countless offerings, what truly reso-nates and leaves an impact is something that's distinct, addressing a gap or fulfilling a need that's yet to be met. After understanding the importance of core values and how they influence our daily interactions and offerings, it's crucial to recognize that for our contributions to truly matter, they must stand out. It's not just about offering something; it's about offering something that's needed, necessary, and unique to you.

Throughout my years of working in HR, I have become familiar with several of its varying functions, such as talent acquisition, training and development, benefits, and compensation, but much of my experience has been in employee relations (ER) and labor relations (LR). ER takes a reactive approach, addressing people problems as they arise in the workplace, supporting both leaders and employees alike. LR, too, is typically reactionary, managing labor union relations and grievances, often only stepping in when there are labor union matters.

Working in both areas, I started to recognize a substantial "white space" within HR. In business terms, white space commonly refers to unexplored or overlooked segments within an existing domain, where a particular product or service has yet to make its mark. Such unexplored spaces serve as fertile ground for growth and innovative enhancements, where introducing something previously nonexistent—yet necessary—becomes possible. With minimal to no competition, these areas provide an opportunity to establish a presence and exert dominance.

I came to understand that there was not a unique segment within HR dedicated to proactively spotting potential workplace problems before they grew into ER or LR challenges. By the time these departments stepped in, an issue had already surfaced. This sparked a thought: *What if we could catch these problems early on before they became widespread workplace issues?* Could we put in place a proactive process to evaluate workplace environments, pinpoint challenges, and train others to do the same, consequently dealing with potential issues before they escalate?

Upon uncovering this significant gap in HR, I was able to introduce this concept to my leader Rob, and was given the green light to run with it. After a few years, I had the opportunity to kickstart programs and initiatives for several companies and recognized that I had cultivated a unique skill set in an area where formal guidelines didn't exist. I inadvertently carved out my unique space within the industry to become an indispensable asset in the realm of workplace culture. As my proficiency in this unique area grew increasingly evident, I noticed a perceptible shift in people's attitudes toward me. The value I brought to the table was no longer just acknowledged; it was actively sought out.

Identifying this white space empowered me to craft concepts so exceptional no one else could replicate them or dictate how they should be done. All they knew was that my offering was a necessity. Most businesses traditionally function with a reactive mindset, reaching out to HR for assistance only when an issue has already erupted. However, my company sought to revolutionize this way of thinking, shifting the business mindset from "There's a workplace problem; I need HR help" to "I want to avoid potential problems; let's contact an HR consultant." The HR Plug is not just for putting out fires but working proactively to prevent them. This mindset shift allowed me to dominate this white space by providing solutions that set both me and my firm apart in the business landscape.

I now extend a challenge to you: seek out your own white space—that realm of possibility that awaits your unique gifts, skills, and perspective. Where can you introduce unprecedented value within your sphere of expertise? Often, our greatest innovations spring from our deepest frustrations. Start there. Look closely at what irks you most because hidden within that discomfort is a solution only you can bring to light. And once you discover your white space, brace yourself for an unconventional kind of exhaustion—the one that surprisingly fuels your energy rather than depleting it.

◇◇◇◇◇◇◇◇◇◇◇◇◇◇◇◇◇◇◇◇◇◇◇◇◇◇◇◇◇◇◇◇◇◇◇◇

Once you discover your white space, brace yourself for an unconventional kind of exhaustion—the one that surprisingly fuels your energy rather than depleting it.

A NEW KIND OF EXHAUSTION

Specializing in a niche meant working in a space, possessing insights and solutions that others might only wish they had. This presented its own intensified set of challenges. As a Black woman now leading workplace culture initiatives, I found myself advising senior leaders and shedding light on uncomfortable truths. The irony of the situation was evident: here was a Black woman in the corporate world offering vital feedback, boldly pointing out areas of improvement. The idea that their well-established strategies might have flaws, pointed out by someone they might have perceived as less experienced, was difficult for some to digest. These moments underscored the persistent implicit biases still present, even when the expertise and value are evident.

I quickly became aware of a dual battle I faced with working in this white space. While my expertise was undeniable, it often felt over-shadowed by societal stigmas that questioned my right to be in that space. Every meeting, every presentation, every recommendation was an uphill climb. It wasn't just about the content of my work; it was about breaking down barriers of doubt and skepticism. The weight of constantly proving my worth against a backdrop of subtle and not-so-subtle prejudices became a source of exhausting fatigue.

In my line of work, exhaustion became a constant companion. Yet, the fire and adrenaline rush of transformational change fueled me. I recognized my mission to transform workplace dysfunction and create healthy workplace experiences as my unique Value Offering. I was certain of my purpose; this was what I was created to do. While I knew I needed to persevere and press on, I wrestled with how much more I could endure.

And then one day, during one of those weary moments, I received a profound realization: this taxing journey was a clear indication that I was on a path ordained by God. I suddenly found solace in the thought that God, in His infinite wisdom, doesn't hand out light assignments. He doesn't call us to tasks easily managed by the everyday person. Instead, His assignments come with weight, demanding an unparalleled level of faith and resilience. He trusted me with uncharted territories because He created me with the stamina and brilliance to traverse through them; I was built for this. And all I could do was begin to thank Him for trusting me. And in that moment, I took a step that many overlook—I sought God for clarity on the "how."

It's a common misconception that it is wrong to question or seek understanding from God. Yet, biblical narratives show us that seeking understanding from God is a part of spiritual dialogue. In fact, throughout the Bible, many individuals sought clarity from God regarding their divinely appointed assignments. Moses questioned his ability to lead the Israelites out of Egypt and sought guidance on what to say to them (Exodus 3-4). Gideon, unsure of God's call to save Israel from the Midianites, asked for signs to confirm his mission (Judges 6). And in the New Testament, Ananias hesitated when he was told to meet

Saul, a known persecutor, but God provided the necessary clarity and assurance (Acts 9:10-16). Each of these instances underscores the legitimacy of seeking God's clarity when faced with significant assignments. Asking God about the details is not about questioning His supreme authority but ensuring that we're in alignment with His intentions. Just as biblical figures sought this same type of understanding, we too can approach God with our questions, trusting Him to lead us clearly.

◇◇◇◇◇◇◇◇◇◇◇◇◇◇◇◇◇◇◇◇◇◇◇◇◇◇◇◇◇◇◇◇◇◇◇

God doesn't just show us our destination; He also provides the directions for the journey. We just have to ask.

While many of us understand what God wants from us, the challenge arises when weariness sets in. But stopping isn't the solution. The work remains. The real task lies in partnering with God, seeking His direction on how to move forward. Our misstep often is in thinking we must figure it all out on our own. Instead, if we turn to Him, He provides not just the goal but the path to achieve it. Without His guidance, we might find ourselves working hard but missing the mark. God doesn't just show us our destination; He also provides the directions for the journey. We just have to ask. So, I sought guidance: *Lord, how do I continue to love what I do and stay true to myself? How do I find the strength to rise above negativity? How do I remain Your light in a realm so resistant to change?* It was through these inquiries that I found my answer—start a consulting company. And this blossomed into the business strategy for The HR Plug.

Stepping into the realm of entrepreneurship under God's guidance has reshaped my understanding of exhaustion. My assignment with The HR

Plug is still exhausting. However, this work, while demanding, has introduced a new kind of exhaustion, one that feels purposeful and gratifying. This isn't the draining fatigue from having to defend my legitimacy or expertise; it is the invigorating tiredness that comes from creating, innovating, and transforming. It is the weariness we feel after a day of fruitful labor, knowing that seeds have been sown and will soon bear much fruit. This exhaustion, in its divine design, wasn't about depleting my energy but about refining and building my strength, molding me for the purpose God envisioned. While this path is demanding, every challenge, every late night, every brainstorming session, and every new connection adds layers to my growth and brings me closer to God's purpose.

Now, whenever I feel the sting of hurt or annoyance from criticisms and misunderstandings creep in, I take that as a sign that God still trusts me. And I think about the colossal mission that God assigned to Jesus. If Jesus, in His divine love, bore such an immense burden, who was I to flinch from these trivial challenges? My tiny suffering doesn't even compare to His sacrifice and endurance. This is why the apostle Paul reminds us in 1 Corinthians 15:31 that we must die daily. It's a testament to the daily sufferings, sacrifices, and commitment that will be needed to persevere and fulfill God's purpose and that the responsibility for determining the methods lies with Him, not solely with us. These tasks require us to let go of our personal desires daily, embracing the larger purpose He has set for us.

YOUR VALUE OFFERINGS MAKE YOU INDISPENSABLE

Embracing your divine assignment requires a shift in your mindset—it's about prioritizing God's will above your own. Once you fully embrace your divine assignment and surrender to God with an unwavering "yes," you've effectively placed His desires above your own. It then becomes less about your own perceptions of feasibility and more about your unwavering trust in Him. Remember, God values your obedience and will never leave you hanging when you walk in His will. The strategies you seek, the solutions you desire, they all flow from Him. When you prioritize God's purpose, He equips and guides you every step of the way.

◇◇◇◇◇◇◇◇◇◇◇◇◇◇◇◇◇◇◇◇◇◇◇◇◇◇◇◇◇◇◇◇◇◇

Embracing your divine assignment requires a shift in your mindset—it's about prioritizing God's will above your own.

When I accepted my calling, seeing it as God's tailored plan for me, I turned to Him for every solution and insight. This led many to ask, "How did you know to approach it this way or solve that challenge?" And, honestly, I was often at a loss for words. The solutions felt instinctive to me. In retrospect now, however, it all makes sense. Strategy is my Organic Brilliance; it flows effortlessly from me. Advocacy, on the other hand, is a core value that's deeply ingrained in my belief system. So, it only stands to reason that my unique contribution centers on devising strategies that champion causes or stand up for individuals. I have nestled into the mold, fitting seamlessly into the plan God crafted just for me.

True indispensability stems from the singular melding of one's distinct identity and innate attributes, combined with the unparalleled way one leverages these traits to offer value. It's about presenting an irreplaceable perspective, a standout skill, or an unmatched methodology. It's the pursuit of excellence that leaves an imprint, making people instinctively link your name with reliability and quality. Most crucially, it's carving out such a distinctive and invaluable niche that others find it hard to envision reaching their aspirations without your input.

I've embraced an exercise that has not only helped me discern my Value Offering but also pinpoint areas where others view me as indispensable. Here's what I'd recommend you try: Reach out to at least five individuals in your life, spanning friends, colleagues, and family. Pose this question to them: "What is the one thing you feel I excel at so much that you wouldn't want to do it without me?" As you gather responses, pay close attention to the areas of consensus. These overlapping qualities can reveal where your involvement is crucial for others. Reflect on these commonalities. With a bit of focus and fine-tuning, you could leverage these areas to carve out a new pathway for yourself—a path where your refined expertise renders you truly indispensable.

Your distinct abilities are the hallmarks of your greatness. It's imperative to stand confident in who you are, even when faced with misunderstandings and detractors. My journey, like yours, has been fraught with challenges aiming to shake your belief in your own potential. In such times, firmly anchor yourself in your identity and remain vigilant against detours designed to sidetrack you. Draw strength from Isaiah 54:17 (AMP):

> *"No weapon that is formed against you will succeed; And every tongue that rises against you in judgment you will condemn. This [peace, righteousness, security, and triumph over opposition] is the heritage of the servants of the LORD, And this is their vindication from Me," says the LORD.*

Let this be a reminder that your journey, despite the challenges, is under divine protection and marked for victory.

MINISTRY IN THE MARKETPLACE

I've come to realize that my profession, my expertise, is more than just a job; it's a "Ministry in the Marketplace." The work I do, the value I bring, is infused with a higher purpose. *The marketplace* represents the global arena where we conduct business, where opportunities are seized, ideas are traded, and relationships are forged. While I might not be seated in the traditional role of pastor, prophet, or evangelist, I recognize that I am navigating a divine ministry. Every consultation, every strategy, every interaction is a manifestation of God's work, and it's an avenue through which I can exemplify His love, especially in a world that seems to have an affinity for its opposite. It's my way of serving Him, of letting His light shine through in unexpected places.

Just as I've found my Ministry in the Marketplace, I believe you, too, have a unique ministry waiting for you there. Remember, our call is not just to reach those already familiar with God's love but to shine brightly for those yet to encounter it. God has handpicked and honed your skills, talents, and passions to create an offering that resonates in the hearts and lives of those around you. It's an offering meant to uplift, inspire, and, above all, please the One who designed it. When you align your professional life, or any part of your life for that matter, with this truth, your work becomes more than just tasks and goals. It becomes a ministry, a worship, and a testament to the God-given value that is uniquely yours.

◇◇◇◇◇◇◇◇◇◇◇◇◇◇◇◇◇◇◇◇◇◇◇◇◇◇◇◇◇◇◇◇◇◇◇◇◇◇◇

God has handpicked and honed your skills, talents, and passions to create an offering that resonates in the hearts and lives of those around you. It's an offering meant to uplift, inspire, and, above all, please the One who designed it.

Ministry in the Marketplace transcends the traditional concept that ministry is confined within the four walls of a church. It takes the message of hope and grace out into the world, reaching people who might never set foot in a church. It's important to remember that the Bible teaches us that we, as believers, are the true church (2 Corinthians 6:16). The *church* isn't merely a physical structure but comprises individuals who have committed their lives to Jesus Christ. As we prioritize God's purpose in our careers and daily lives, we inadvertently become representations of His light in professional, social, and even casual settings. In doing so, we're gifted with greater influence and opportunities to reflect His love and character.

MARKETPLACE MINISTRY: REFLECTING CHRIST IN EVERYDAY INTERACTIONS

We're in a season where we must meet people right where they are, fostering connections through relatability to establish genuine relationships. This is reminiscent of Paul's adaptability in his ministry:

To the weak I became weak, to win the weak. I have become all things to all people so that by all possible means I might save some. I do all this for the sake of the gospel, that I may share in its blessings. —1 Corinthians 9:22–23 (NIV)

Paul's teachings emphasize the importance of empathizing with those we work and interact with, allowing us to embody and extend the love Christ has for us more effectively. By living out the love Christ has shown us and adhering to the virtues He teaches, we can truly represent what it means to be genuine believers. Acting in harmony with the fruit of the Spirit and using His truths to guide our actions, we act as light in a world full of darkness.

Observing this transformative grace in our lives can inspire others to seek the same fulfilling and enriching path we've chosen. Your gifts and talents, when executed with excellence, can pique the curiosity of others, making them wonder about the source of your passion and skill. It's an invitation, an open door, to share the deeper purpose and love that drives you. So, take a moment to reflect on your daily interactions and responsibilities in your place of work. How can you infuse them with purpose, grace, and intentionality, turning ordinary moments into opportunities for ministry?

When we speak of *ministry*, it's not about brandishing a Bible to impose biblical teachings upon others. Rather, it's being a tangible reflection of Christ's love and hope in our everyday actions and interactions. Think of it this way: when faced with the challenge of delivering difficult news at work or in a business transaction, ministry is choosing to communicate with patience and kindness, ensuring the message is delivered with grace. It's about turning everyday tasks into opportunities to radiate Christlike compassion. In this nontraditional form, ministry is defined as the subtle yet powerful embodiment of Christ's attributes in our daily interactions, where the core of His teachings is reflected not through direct scripture quotation but through our behaviors and character.

◇◇◇◇◇◇◇◇◇◇◇◇◇◇◇◇◇◇◇◇◇◇◇◇◇◇◇◇◇◇◇◇◇

Your gifts and talents, when executed with excellence, can pique the curiosity of others, making them wonder about the source of your passion and skill.

As you go about your tasks and engage with colleagues, clients, or customers, challenge yourself to see beyond the surface. Recognize the potential for ministry in every conversation, every project, and every challenge. Ask yourself, *How can I reflect Christ's love and hope right here, right now, making my workplace a ministry of His light?*

DISCOVER YOUR VALUE OFFERINGS

For guiding principles or values to truly serve their purpose, they should be expressed as action words—verbs, not nouns. It isn't simply saying, "I have a value of integrity." Integrity isn't the Value Offering; it's the action behind integrity, which is about the commitment to "always do the right thing." It's not about offering "innovation" but encouraging one to "look at the problem from a different angle." By translating our value offerings into verbs, we create a roadmap for action, providing clear directions on how to respond in any given situation.

This list provides steps to guide you in defining your Value Offerings:

1. Revisit Your Chosen Core Value: Begin with the core value you've already identified. For this example, let's use "compassion."

2. Turn It Into a Verb-Driven Commitment: Instead of merely recognizing compassion as a value, focus on the actionable manifestation of that value. Ask yourself: How can I demonstrate this in my daily interactions? This could translate to "actively showing empathy and understanding," thereby giving a dynamic essence to compassion.

3. Visualize Practical Scenarios: Contemplate situations in your professional environment where this commitment can be applied. If, for instance, a colleague is facing challenges, your verb-driven commitment might guide you to approach them, offer a listening ear, and "actively show empathy and understanding" rather than just feeling compassionate internally.

4. Commemorate Your Commitment: To solidify and celebrate your commitment to these actionable Value Offerings, consider methods to remember and uphold them. It could be as simple as keeping a journal where you note down instances where you've lived out your verb-driven commitment or sharing your experiences with others.

5. Discuss and Share: Talk about your commitment with colleagues, friends, or family. Expressing your dedication to "actively showing empathy and understanding" not only reinforces your personal commitment but also might inspire others to do the same.

In embracing this approach, you transform static values into dynamic actions, ensuring your Ministry in the Marketplace is always in motion, always evolving.

chapter 8

PURPOSE: YOUR GREATNESS TELLS A STORY ANCHORED TO SOMEONE'S VICTORY

We've already established our identity as the unique blend of your Organic Brilliance and Inimitable Imprints. And we know that everyone's composition is different, valuable, and necessary for something. That "something" that people are necessary for is called purpose.

◇◇◇◇◇◇◇◇◇◇◇◇◇◇◇◇◇◇◇◇◇◇◇◇◇◇◇◇◇◇◇◇◇

Our existence in this world is not about us; it's about our experiences—the good times, and the tough ones—things that can help others who might be struggling to keep going.

I'm a firm believer that each one of us has a unique purpose. Our existence in this world is not about us; it's about our experiences—the good times, and the tough ones—things that can help others who might be struggling to keep going. When you discover your purpose, it pushes you to do more, to be better. It's about looking at everything you've been through and figuring out what life is trying to teach you. Every single one of us goes through challenging moments in life. Sometimes, these can seem like setbacks or huge hurdles. But here's the real deal: These tough times? They're actually our best teachers. They have this amazing power to push us to learn, grow, and sharpen our skills in ways we might not have thought possible. And, when we look back, we appreciate them for the role they played in our growth.

Our life experiences are the lessons that ultimately transform us from life's students to life's teachers; this is what purpose is about. It's about taking those successful victories or those hard-earned lessons and using them to light the way for others. So, even when it feels like life is throwing curveballs at us, remember this—we're just in a learning phase. Yes, it's hard, and yes, it's uncomfortable. But with every challenge we tackle, we're getting stronger, smarter, and more capable. It's all part of discovering your purpose—figuring out what you're truly meant to do. Now, if we shift our mindset a bit, and start seeing these tough times not as hurdles but as teachers, we're opening a whole new level of personal growth and self-discovery.

YOUR STORY IS TIED TO YOUR PURPOSE

Now, here's an important thing to remember: your purpose is often tied to the moments in your life that had the most impact for you. I'm talking about those times that really rocked your world, pushed you out of your comfort zone, or shook you to your core. That's where your purpose is lurking. So, it's time to think about those moments because they are all chapters of your story.

While I'm sure you probably have a slew of stories, think about the ones that really meant something, that changed something for you. The raw, real pieces of your story that you might even be living through right now. It's these impactful stories, the ones that everyone can't necessarily relate to because they are so uniquely yours, that are often the most compelling routes to discovering your purpose.

This isn't always an easy journey, but it's a crucial one. Because it's not about just finding a purpose, it's about finding the purpose that resonates with your life's deepest experiences. It's about turning your hardest battles into your biggest strengths and using them to make a difference in the lives of others. This is what makes your purpose truly meaningful, and this is what makes you, you.

TRACY'S STORY

Allow me to share Tracy's journey with you—a mentee of mine whose personal story of overcoming has become a source of inspiration for those around her. Tracy is a participant in The Greatness Lab, my mentorship program that helps people understand who they are and discover the life they were created to live. During her self-discovery process, we started talking about her Inimitable Imprints. She shared how she has a noticeable ability to remain composed under stress, to the point where it became a part of her professional reputation. It was a trait that fascinated people. Even amid chaos, Tracy has the ability to remain unmoved, somewhat like a calm port in a storm. Her reactions were so strikingly different from the norm that they became known as "The Tracy Way," a testament to her extraordinary composure.

This, however, wasn't always received positively. Some mistook Tracy's equanimity for indifference. There were instances when others interpreted Tracy's calm demeanor as a lack of emotion, leading them to believe she didn't care. Tracy took this feedback to heart, striving to convey emotions in a way that would satisfy those around her. It was becoming a burdensome task as she dealt with the challenge of fulfilling others' expectations to show emotion that comforted them but left her feeling drained and twisted in discomfort. As an attempt to ease their feelings, Tracy began to alter her true self, all to prevent people from making assumptions about her simply because her reactions deviated from their expectations. While explaining this during our session, she paused and asked me a question. She said, "I can't figure out what I need to do to change this about me. How do I adjust my demeanor so that others know that I do care?" And that's when I had to interrupt and assure her: "There's absolutely nothing wrong with you, Tracy."

We often mistake ourselves for being flawed when others can't quite understand or align with our ways, especially when those people hold positions of power over us.

You see, we often mistake ourselves for being flawed when others can't quite understand or align with our ways, especially when those people hold positions of power over us. However, the truth I wanted Tracy to embrace was that there's nothing inherently wrong with her, and she didn't need to change who she fundamentally is. The facets of Tracy's character that others didn't understand weren't her shortcomings but rather areas that needed better articulation. As she journeyed through this self-discovery process, I assured her she would learn how to express these unique qualities more clearly, helping others appreciate them as part of her strength.

I helped Tracy understand that her demeanor wasn't indicative of a lack of concern. Rather, it was a demonstration of her exercising the power of choice. Tracy had mastered the art of self-regulation and choosing where to direct her energy. She didn't waste time or energy on things she couldn't control; she instead chose to maintain self-regulated peace. I asked Tracy to reflect on her journey to understand how she had reached this point. What was her story, the narrative that had sculpted her into the composed individual others misunderstood while simultaneously admired? As we dove into her past, the revelations were powerful and inspiring.

Tracy opened up about a challenging chapter of her life. She had undergone a bitter divorce from an unstable husband. This tumultuous situation required Tracy to find an inner calm that many found difficult to comprehend. But she needed to maintain this serenity for her children. If she were to lose control, who would be there to support them? She couldn't risk her freedom or mental health by trying to manage a man whose behavior she had no control over. So, Tracy had to devise her own coping strategy. She learned how to retain control over her emotions rather than granting him the power to dictate her reactions. This choice kept her from responding in ways that could have been more harmful than helpful in the long run.

Reflecting on Tracy's past, we recognized how the most challenging period in her life had equipped her with a unique ability that she could now use to help others. The necessity of maintaining calm and composure while going through the process of a divorce from someone who was mentally unstable had fundamentally transformed her. If she had mirrored the behavior of her partner, she realized she wouldn't have progressed, and nothing would have been accomplished.

The demanding circumstances forced Tracy to learn the power of choice and respond in ways that were most beneficial for her well-being. She discovered how to dismiss external expectations about what "caring" should look like. Now, people admire her for this rare quality. In a world where people naturally get swept up in emotions, Tracy stands as an unshakable pillar of calm. She has the remarkable ability to resist feeding into other people's emotional drama, a quality many find hard to emulate. Her unprovoked and composed demeanor is a testament to her strength. It is indeed a gift and one that's become a part of her distinguished identity.

Tracy has found her purpose, which involves guiding others on how to retain control over their emotions, preventing outbursts and impulsive reactions. She assists people in dissecting the root causes of their emotional responses and assessing the potential impact of these emotions on their peace of mind. She helps them understand the power of choice. It took an unforeseen transformation in Tracy's marriage for her to uncover this gift. Now, she uses this personal revelation to help others navigate their emotional landscapes, offering them the tools to maintain composure in even the most challenging situations.

So now, I pose these questions to you: What's your story? What arduous journey have you endured that could potentially act as a lifeline for someone else? Your trials, your triumphs, your lessons learned—they all have the power to inspire and guide others. Reflect on your experiences, consider how they've shaped you, and think about how they might serve to help others. Remember, our most significant challenges often become our most impactful stories, opening doors to influence, connect, and, ultimately, fulfill our purpose.

◇◇◇◇◇◇◇◇◇◇◇◇◇◇◇◇◇◇◇◇◇◇◇◇◇◇◇◇◇◇◇◇◇◇

Our most significant challenges often become our most impactful stories, opening doors to influence, connect, and, ultimately, fulfill our purpose.

IT'S NOT ABOUT YOU

Here's a critical realization to keep in mind—your purpose is not solely about you. It's true that you play a pivotal role in shaping and living out your purpose. But consider this: the triumphs you reap from your struggles, the victories that rise from your status as a "victim," have ripple effects that reach far beyond your personal sphere. They have the potential to influence, to change, and to empower others. Sometimes, your story, your struggle, and your victory can be the very thing that leads someone else to their triumph. That's the incredible power of purpose; it can turn personal trials into communal victories.

So now the question becomes, if it's not about "you," then who are you purposed for? In the business world, some might call this group your "Target Audience." The term Target Audience refers to the consumers we market our products or services to. However, in the realm of purpose, let's tweak our understanding a bit. This target audience isn't necessarily about who you're selling to but rather, who you're speaking to, serving, or impacting.

Think about it this way. Once you've found your purpose and identified your story of triumph from adversity, the next crucial step is figuring out who you're called to. Who are the people who need to hear your story? Who can benefit from your experiences, your insights, and your wisdom? Who are the people whose lives can be positively altered or even transformed by what you have to share? Those are the people you are called to. They form your target audience in the realm of purpose. It's not about selling but about sharing, uplifting, and changing lives.

You are extraordinary, and you have an audience waiting to witness your greatness. There are countless individuals out there who are yearning to hear your story—who need the inspiration, guidance, or solace your experiences can provide. They just haven't discovered you yet. And maybe you already know this. You might already be aware that you have a story to tell. Perhaps you've pinpointed exactly what that story is and what your purpose entails. The challenge for you isn't about discovery; you've already done that part. This is entirely possible, as I've met numerous people who had their stories figured out but felt hindered from sharing them.

So, let's address the obstacles that might be standing in your way. Shame, guilt, embarrassment, or the dread of being judged are powerful emotions that can hold us hostage, silencing our voices and dulling our spark. These feelings may stem from past mistakes, perceived failures, or the parts of our story that we're not proud of. But here's the thing: these are mere tactics deployed by fear, designed to keep you silent and hold you back. Second Timothy 1:7 reminds us, however, that God has not given us a spirit of timidity, cowardice, or fear.

The key is to not let these feelings mute your voice because remember, it's not about you. It's about the countless people who need to hear your story. Let me assure you, these are common feelings and certainly ones that can be overcome. Your experiences, lessons, and journey have equipped you with the power to impact and inspire others. Don't let fear or shame rob you or the world of your unique light.

◇◇◇◇◇◇◇◇◇◇◇◇◇◇◇◇◇◇◇◇◇◇◇◇◇◇◇◇◇◇◇◇◇◇◇

Your experiences, lessons, and journey have equipped you with the power to impact and inspire others. Don't let fear or shame rob you or the world of your unique light.

LET YOUR STORY UNFOLD

There's a woman whom I've come to greatly admire, and I'd like to share a bit of her journey with you. As a young girl of just thirteen, she found herself pregnant, stepping into the role of a mother. She had her baby at the age of fourteen and graduated high school early, only to drop out of college in her pursuit to fend for herself and her child. She ended up waitressing at a strip club. Her life was marred by a relationship that was emotionally abusive, leading her to a premature marriage at nineteen. The vows didn't hold, and by the age of twenty-three, she was divorced.

In the aftermath of this tumultuous period, she battled the demons of low self-esteem, depression, guilt, and shame. All of this—the hardship, pain, and struggle—are part of her story. To help her get through these tough times in life, she started blogging. She poured her feelings, thoughts, and experiences onto the page, sharing her raw emotions with the world. Her openness resonated deeply with people, leading to a surge in followers who started sharing their own stories, their own struggles, and their own victories with her.

Her voice, once merely a whisper lost in the noise, became a safe space of familiarity and assurance that those hearing her story were not alone in their struggles. As people started responding in gratitude, she realized that there were others out there, broken and yearning for healing, and she had a part to play in their journey. Through this process, she began to find the power in her story and the impact it could have in helping others find their path to healing. This interaction and exchange of experiences led to a profound revelation for her—she discovered her purpose.

The transformation wasn't an overnight feat. From a fearful and insecure young girl, she morphed into a powerhouse figure of strength and inspiration. The "she" in this story is Sarah Jakes Roberts—a celebrated author, influential speaker, and copastor of The Potter's House at One LA and The Potter's House Denver, alongside her husband, Touré Roberts. She is a wife, mother, businesswoman, and leader who has defined her purpose as utilizing "her experiences, insight, and influence to help every soul she encounters to evolve into the best version of themselves."

So, when we talk about the process of finding your purpose, it's about embracing the entirety of your journey. Your story, no matter how filled with trials and tribulations, is a tool for change. It's a source of hope and resilience, not just for you but potentially for countless others. Sarah Jakes Roberts is a prime example of this transformative power. She deserves immense respect for her bravery, tenacity, and compassion. From the ashes of her past, she has risen to inspire and lead, impacting countless lives, all because she told her story.

THE WRITING STARTS NOW

My seventeen-year-old daughter has a dream: she wants to be a pilot. To get a head start, she's juggling her high school work and an aviation program at our local community college. The day she started her dual enrollment program at the college, I got a text from her. It read, *Mom, I'm the only girl in the class.*

At that moment, I knew this was going to be the beginning of a journey, a part of her story. I could only respond with encouragement, reminding her of that, so I texted her back, urging her to keep track of these experiences. I told her, *Write down how it feels to be the only girl in a room full of boys who want the same dream as you. This is just a part of your story. I'll explain more when you get home.* That afternoon, I told her to watch how this story unfolds. Each step she takes in this male-dominated field, she's not just walking toward her dream but also creating a story that might inspire someone else tomorrow.

Crafting your story isn't like a school assignment, where you plan an introduction, plot, climax, and conclusion. Instead, your story is knitted together by the moments that unfold along your journey. That's why it's so crucial to chronicle these episodes of your life, however you choose to do it. Whether through a journal, a blog, a vlog, or audio recordings, these tools can serve as a time capsule for your experiences. Each note, each entry, becomes a building block in the narrative of your life. Recording these moments in real-time allows you to preserve the rawness, the authenticity, and the immediacy. And when looped together, they create a quilt of lessons, experiences, and wisdom to share with others in the future. Your story isn't just for you, it's a guide for someone else navigating their own journey. So, start recording your moments, your chapters, and let your story begin to unfold.

It's time to shatter your silence and unleash your Greatness into the world. There are people out there who need you and a purpose waiting for you to step into it. So, here's a challenge for you: Dedicate one entire, undisturbed hour every day, solely to focus on you. In this time, engage with your innermost self. And because God is within you, you're intrinsically communing with Him as well. This isn't a time for prayer—prayer is our opportunity to talk to God. Instead, this is your moment to listen, to become receptive to His messages for you. The way you embrace God, His path, His intentions, and His love shapes the clarity and frequency with which you'll hear from Him.

What are you seeking clarity on about your purpose? Your audience? Your story? Jot these questions down, and during your daily designated "Me Time," wait for His responses. The more time you allot solely to Him, the more you'll begin to discern His voice. He is eager to share with you the insights about who He created you to be.

Commit to this one hour a day, stick to it for at least thirty days, jotting down what you hear, and watch your story start to unravel before your eyes. Sarah Jakes Roberts tells her story in her book *Lost and Found: Finding Hope in the Detours of Life.* When she was asked in an interview about the reactions she received from people after sharing her story, she said, "They read my story and tell me that they see so much of themselves in me, while others tell me that although they weren't a teen mom, they still identified with how I had low self-esteem. People are seeing bits and pieces of themselves in the story."

LIVE IN PURPOSE

It's easy to feel downhearted when faced with life's obstacles. Still, it's vital to understand that these challenges exist not to break us but to build us for what's ahead. The lessons we learn from these testing times can become lifelines for others who may lack the strength to overcome similar situations. So, instead of wallowing in self-pity on these occasions, get up! Embrace them. Train your mind to face the challenge and get curious to wonder about what God is trying to teach you, build you for, or prepare you for because elevation isn't granted; it's earned, and it rarely comes without sacrifice.

As you journal, highlight the significance of documenting both setbacks and victories, ensuring that you don't lose sight of the essential details. Every patch of the quilt matters—no part is too trivial or monumental to contribute to the grand picture of your life story.

Understand that you're living this life because you're not only made as Greatness but you're also chosen for something greater. God has immeasurably more planned for you, exceeding what you can even fathom. There are several passages of scripture that reaffirm this: You are chosen, as stated in 1 Peter 2:9. You have been set apart, specially gifted, prepared (1 John 2:20), and called for a special purpose (1 Corinthians 12). You have been adopted, appointed, and purposefully planted (John 15:16) in this life.

◇◇◇◇◇◇◇◇◇◇◇◇◇◇◇◇◇◇◇◇◇◇◇◇◇◇◇◇◇◇

You're living your life because you're not only made as Greatness but you're also chosen for something greater.

Hold these truths close to your heart and step into the extraordinary destiny that awaits you. Step forward in faith, guided by purpose, and fueled by the knowledge that you are chosen, unique, and equipped with everything you need to impact the world. This is what living in your purpose is all about.

VISION

chapter 9

PLAN:
YOUR GREATNESS DESIGNED
BY THE DECADE

E very January, as we ring in a new year, my social media feed predictably overflows with posts about vision board parties. If you've never been to a vision board party, imagine being in a room full of enthusiastic individuals ready to visually map out their aspirations for the year ahead. They flip through magazines, looking for images and phrases to cut out that resonate with their goals. These crafted boards stand as vibrant reminders to inspire what they hope to achieve for the year ahead.

The dictionary defines a vision board as "a collage of images and words representing a person's wishes or goals, intended to serve as inspiration or motivation." At their core, vision boards are deeply personal. There's no set playbook on their creation—no fixed size, shape, or timeline. The real essence lies in crafting something that resonates with you, something that stirs inspiration and motivation daily.

However, given the annual buzz every January—with everyone seemingly hosting or attending these parties—it's clear that for many, vision boards have become a yearly ritual. Traditionally, we've approached vision boards as a year-long blueprint, a snapshot of the next twelve months. But is that the best approach? I can't shake the feeling that we might be limiting ourselves. To me, a genuine vision shouldn't be confined to just a year. Why not dare to dream bigger, charting out not just the next year but the next ten or twenty years? Think about the power of shaping a vision that carries you well beyond the now. Have you ever thought about where you see yourself in the next 10 years instead of simply next year?

VISION: PLANNING THE UNSEEN

Often, when we hear the word "vision," our minds automatically translate it into mere goals or ambitions. Some might even think it's just a fleeting daydream, a whimsical moment where they picture themselves somewhere in the distant future. But the concept of vision, especially in the context of life and the predestined future, is far more profound than that.

Think of vision as a guiding star on your life's journey. It's not just about what you want to achieve but how you envision the whole journey unfolding. Every aspiration, every deep-seated desire you have, finds its place in this vision. More than just hopes and dreams, your vision lays out a clear path to how you want your future to look. It's the framework for your life's master plan, illuminating the way to your desired outcomes.

A vision is the blueprint of your life, tailor-made to fuel your purpose. It's about creating a life on your terms, harmonized with your deeper calling. You see, once you discover your purpose, it becomes a source of boundless inspiration, flooding you with ideas. As ideas start pouring in, each more exciting than the last, you'll be eager to create a vision to set them all into motion. But here's the catch: without a solid blueprint, these brilliant ideas that create this "desirable future" for you will remain just that—ideas. Without thoughtful planning and a solid structure, your ideas won't pan out as you had hoped, and that spark of enthusiasm will quickly dim into frustration. There's no doubt that purpose attracts vision, but a vision without a plan is just a dream.

Recall our discussion about your story. Shaped by both struggles and successes, your story resonates with a purpose deeper than you might realize. It serves as a compass, pointing to those you're destined to guide and those who seek the wisdom you've acquired. Recognizing the link between your story and its purpose is a pivotal moment, but it's merely a starting point. It's your vision that creates the path that takes you to the finish line. Vision is the momentum that drives your purpose, the canvas for your story, setting you on course to resonate with the very hearts you're meant to touch.

◇◇◇◇◇◇◇◇◇◇◇◇◇◇◇◇◇◇◇◇◇◇◇◇◇◇◇◇◇◇◇◇◇

It's your vision that creates the path that takes you to the finish line and drives your purpose, the canvas for your story, setting you on course to resonate with the very hearts you're meant to touch.

Rooted in our deepest ambitions, your vision serves as the guiding force that brings your desires from the realm of dreams into reality.

With a clear, compelling vision, we have a roadmap—one that directs our choices, fuels our passion, and holds the power to shape our imagined future.

GOALS VS. VISION: THINK BIGGER

At first glance, the terms "goal" and "vision" might appear interchangeable. It's common to hear people express their ambitions using both words, whether it's, "I have a goal to become the CEO of my own company," or "My vision is to be the CEO of my company one day." On the surface, both statements convey a similar aspiration. Yet, when we look deeper, there's a nuanced difference between the two concepts, and understanding this distinction can significantly impact your journey toward success.

Goals are specific, measurable steps we set to achieve larger aspirations. They aren't broad ambitions like "becoming the CEO of my own company" but rather the actionable steps taken to eventually pave the way to becoming the CEO of your own company. Goals serve as indicators by creating immediate tasks to ensure we stay on course toward fulfilling our vision. So, if I aspire to become a CEO, a goal I set might read: "To enhance my leadership capabilities, I'll complete two leadership courses within the next quarter." This statement is an example of a clear, actionable goal that drives momentum toward making my desire to become a CEO happen.

A vision, on the other hand, is the big picture, a long-term view of where you imagine yourself in the future. It is more abstract, encompassing not just what you aim to achieve but also why you want to achieve it and how it aligns with your core values and purpose. A vision acts as a guiding light, giving our purpose an assignment. When someone says, "My vision is to be the CEO of my company one day," they are not simply referring to a job or title. They are showing an ultimate desire to lead, influence, and make significant decisions that align with their personal and professional aspirations.

◇◇◇◇◇◇◇◇◇◇◇◇◇◇◇◇◇◇◇◇◇◇◇◇◇◇◇◇◇◇◇◇◇

Goals are the steps we take; vision is the destination we're walking toward. Goals are the means to an end, while the vision is the end itself.

In simpler terms, while goals are the steps we take, vision is the destination we're walking toward. Goals are the means to an end, while the vision is the end itself. It's vital to grasp this differentiation because, without a vision, our goals can become disconnected and lack a unifying purpose. On the flip side, having a vision without setting goals can leave us feeling adrift, unsure of how to bring our aspirations to life. Together, however, vision and goals form a potent combination, a roadmap that not only tells us where we're headed but also how to get there while measuring our progress along the way.

As you continue down this self-discovery journey and begin creating the vision for your future, pause and reflect: Is what you're calling a "vision" truly that expansive aspiration? Or is it simply a goal, subtly limiting your potential? To truly harness the power of vision, you need to think bigger, beyond immediate objectives. Your vision is the overarching story of your future; it's about plotting that far-reaching destination for the next ten to twenty years. Goals? They're the chapters, the actionable steps leading to that grand finale. So, when you're sketching out your life's desires, ensure you're not just planning for the immediate. Stretch your boundaries. Dream audaciously. Think bigger.

CRAFTING YOUR VISION: A BOOK WITH DISTINCT CHAPTERS

Thinking bigger requires the courage to craft a vision that may initially seem overwhelming. Remember, each challenge you've faced, every setback you've endured, served to fortify you, equipping you to bear the weight of your vision. Those moments of trials, those battles, were never solely about you. Instead, they were catalysts, shaping and molding what's birthing out of you. Just as the birth of a larger baby can mean more intense labor pains, you had to go through what you went through because you carry a monumental purpose. It's the overcoming and endurance of these experiences that brought you to this point. Having persevered and emerged stronger, it's now time for the vision to be born.

I understand that contemplating what's next might feel scary. The magnitude of it all can be overwhelming. But James 5:11 (AMP) reminds us, "We call those blessed [happy, spiritually prosperous, favored by God] who were steadfast *and* endured [difficult circumstances]." Your perseverance through your difficulties has earned you divine favor. This is precisely why it's crucial to remember and embrace every facet of your being: your Organic Brilliance, your Inimitable Imprints, your Distinguished Identity, your values and beliefs, your story and purpose. Drawing strength from this profound self-awareness is your key to living the life you were created to live.

Given the expansive nature of a vision, breaking it down into more digestible segments makes writing your life plan much more manageable. Segmenting it into more digestible parts presents a structure to write it out as your life plan for the next decade. I like to call these segments "chapters" in what I like to call your "Book of Visions: Your Imagined Future by the Decade." Each chapter zeroes in on a specific aspect of your life that you will envision your imagined future for. You will write a life plan for each chapter that will contribute and align with your overarching vision. Visualize this process like creating a quilt: every chapter symbolizes a unique patch, and once sewn together, they collectively manifest a blanket that vividly portrays your full vision.

Your perseverance through your difficulties has earned you divine favor. This is precisely why it's crucial to remember and embrace every facet of your being.

WRITING YOUR BOOK OF VISIONS

The act of writing down a vision is far more powerful than merely holding it in our minds. While it might feel sufficient to "know it," the tangible act of writing solidifies, clarifies, and commits us to our aspirations. There's a profound reason the Bible instructs us on this very principle. Habakkuk 2:2 (AMP) tells us, "Write the vision and engrave it plainly on [clay] tablets so that the one who reads it will run." This is such a powerful revelation. As we dissect this scripture, allow me to share the intention behind the instruction to "write the vision."

The scripture states, "Write the vision and engrave it plainly on clay tablets." Here, the "tablet" is not just any surface but represents a slab of stone-like material used as a writing medium. During biblical times, whatever was written on a tablet was engraved or impressed into it to document and preserve the message. So, God isn't merely suggesting we scribble this down casually; He's instructing us to pen it with purpose, emphasizing its profound importance.

The latter part of the scripture resonates equally, emphasizing "so that the one who reads it will run." Engraving demands deliberation and care, so writing your vision should also. It should be read in such a way that anyone who sees it instinctively understands it, with no room for misinterpretations or second guesses. Remember, your vision isn't solely for your benefit; it's an assignment given to you to fulfill others' destinies too.

Commit your vision to paper, not just as a record but as a bold declaration of its importance and your unwavering covenant to its realization. As Oprah Winfrey wisely stated, "Create the highest, grandest vision possible for your life because you become what you believe." Stand tall in your belief, and watch as you masterfully lead your destiny to live the extraordinary life you were created to live.

MAPPING OUT THE CHAPTERS

Breaking your vision into chapters illuminates a direct path to the future you imagine. With each chapter, you'll explore every corner of your life with clarity and purpose. As you begin to write each chapter, you'll unravel detailed layers of your life, set intentional goals, and tap into the deeper currents that fuel your purpose. The outcome? A thoroughly constructed life plan for each chapter, written with insightful intention. Together, these chapters form the pages of your Book of Visions, offering a comprehensive life plan.

Below are the defined chapters for which you'll shape your life plan. As you delve into each chapter description, ask yourself: *What do I desire this area of my life to look like 10 years from now?*

LIFE PLAN CHAPTERS:
◇ Health and Wellness: This pertains to physical health, mental well-being, and overall lifestyle habits. A vision in this area can focus on fitness goals, dietary changes, mental health strategies, and more.

◇ Family: This involves relationships with immediate family, extended family, and even chosen family. The vision can include strengthening bonds, creating family traditions, or planning for a growing family.

◇ Finances: This is about financial security, growth, investments, and future planning. It can encompass saving strategies, investment goals, and milestones like buying a house or retiring comfortably.

◇ Spiritual Growth: This can vary greatly from person to person. It might include deepening your religious faith, exploring spiritual practices, or seeking personal growth and enlightenment.

◇ Professional Development: This is centered on career advancement, skill acquisition, networking, and achieving specific job-related milestones. It can also delve into entrepreneurial endeavors or changing career paths.

◇ Me (Self-Love): This is where you are intentionally investing in yourself. It can cover personal growth, hobbies, activities for relaxation and rejuvenation, travel, a bucket list, or other types of personal milestones.

◇ Social Engagements: Relationships outside of family, like friendships and community involvement are included here. This could involve deepening current friendships, building new ones, or becoming more involved in local or global communities.

◇ Knowledge Attainment: This includes lifelong learning goals, whether it's formal education, taking courses, attending workshops, or self-study.

◇ Legacy: How you'd like to be remembered, the impact you want to make on the world, or the legacy you want to leave behind.

CRAFTING VISION STATEMENTS BY DECADE

For each chapter listed, you'll want to start focusing on crafting vision statements. A vision statement is a concise, clearly defined sentence that vividly captures where you hope to be in the next 10 years. You should plan to have only 1-2 vision statements for each chapter. Remember, your statement doesn't have to be convoluted or complicated; keep it simple and plain. To get started, you can use this template to help with structuring your writing: "In 10 years, when I think about my [chapter name], I will . . ." and then complete this thought with a description of your aspiration for that specific area. This format will serve as a guide, ensuring concise clarity for your intended outcome.

Consider this as an example: If you were writing a vision statement for the Health and Wellness chapter, it might read, "In 10 years, when I think about my Health and Wellness, I will be leading a balanced lifestyle, complete with regular exercise five times a week and mindful eating habits." This is what a well-crafted vision statement should look like. It doesn't matter if you come up with one statement or two; it's solely about capturing a reasonably defined desire. The key is to consider each statement as a micro-vision for that area, thinking well beyond writing just a goal.

Focus on writing all your vision statements for each chapter first. Write them out, listed by chapter with, your 1-2 bullets beneath sharing the micro-vision. Read it aloud. Spend some time meditating on it, praying over it, and asking God about it. This is a 10-year commitment you're making, so alignment to your purpose planted in your identity is of utmost importance. Once you have your vision statements in place, you can then shift your focus to breaking down each statement by constructing impactful goals to bring these vision statements to life.

GOODBYE GOALS, HELLO MILESTONES

Until now, I've consistently referred to the term "goals" when discussing the measurable steps we'll take to realize each vision statement. I chose goals primarily for their familiarity and comprehensibility. Introducing the idea that goals might not be the best fit before laying out the entire process could have muddied the waters. However, now that we've delved deeper into devising our life plan, it's essential to refine our terminology: what we've been referring to as goals will now be more accurately referred to as "milestones."

◇◇◇◇◇◇◇◇◇◇◇◇◇◇◇◇◇◇◇◇◇◇◇◇◇◇◇◇◇◇◇

Because our life plan is a journey, not a project, the most appropriate measuring indicator would be establishing milestones rather than goals.

Because our life plan is a journey, not a project, the most appropriate measuring indicator would be establishing milestones rather than goals. Goals are best suited for project or experimental settings where there are a clear endpoint and a structured process, allowing for specific, quantifiable targets to be set and met. In contrast, our life's journey is fluid, evolving, and continuous, making it imperative to measure our progress in stages rather than end objectives. In this journey, our stages of measurement are time-bound, with each stage being reflective of one year. This annual plan allows for a strategic pause to assess and adjust, ensuring we remain aligned with our 10-year chapter vision statement.

Milestones provide the adaptability we need for this voyage. They'll give us the flexibility to celebrate progress, adjust to life's unpredictable turns, and stay motivated toward our overarching vision. Think of it like climbing a mountain: while reaching the peak is the ultimate desire, it's the base camps along the climb—each a milestone—that allow climbers to rest, evaluate their journey, adapt to conditions, and ensure they are on the right path to the top.

As we finalize the formulation of our vision statements for each chapter of our life, it becomes pivotal to turn our attention to milestones. These milestones serve as our compass, ensuring we remain committed and take the necessary steps to realize our visions. By determining the stages for these milestones, you'll gain clarity on what needs to be achieved and by when. Remember, we're working with a 10-year timeframe. Let's revisit the Health and Wellness chapter vision statement example where we said, "In 10 years, when I think about my Health and Wellness, I will be leading a balanced lifestyle, complete with regular exercise five times a week and mindful eating habits." That's the broad picture. Our next step? Crafting milestones to methodically guide us toward manifesting that envisioned future.

CRAFTING VISION MILESTONES: THE 4-STEP PROCESS

By translating your broader vision statements into milestones, you create a roadmap filled with clear landmarks, leading you toward the realization of your aspirations. To achieve this, we'll adopt a systematic approach, walking you through each step to ensure a detailed yet actionable pathway.

STEP 1: DISSECTING THE VISION

The process begins by breaking down your vision statement into its core components, diving into the essence and purpose behind each aspect of your broader vision. Your aim is to identify the main themes native to your vision. Think of this process as isolating the vital ingredients in a complex recipe. Using our established example, if your vision is centered on "leading a balanced life with regular exercise and mindful eating habits," you can break this down into the components of exercise consistency, exercise types, dietary habits, and mental balance.

STEP 2: DETERMINING THE "HOW"

Next, we'll question the methodology behind each component to understand how you plan to target each element for the first year. By narrowing down this timeframe, we can channel our energy and establish a solid foundation for progressive growth. Each year's subsequent strategies will organically build upon the last, ensuring a consistent stride toward realizing your 10-year vision.

Then, we will take each component to define "how" you will focus on that specific area for the year. Your "hows" that are identified will be your overall strategy for the year. Continuing with our previous example, for the component "exercise consistency," framing your "hows" might look like:

◇ "How frequently will I exercise to meet the target?"

◇ "How long do I envision each exercise session lasting?"

◇ "How will I integrate exercising into my weekday schedule?"

Each "how" question serves to guide your focus, pinpointing the specific target related to the broader components of your vision statement. You may not necessarily use them all in the next step.

STEP 3: DETAILING THE ACTION

In this essential step, you'll turn your strategy from Step 2 into concrete actions. By zeroing in on quarterly objectives, you establish a rhythm of continual growth and achievement. This steady, structured method guarantees each quarter propels you forward, building on the success of the previous one. For each quarter, you'll pinpoint a specific focus and action that supports your overarching strategy.

Here's what this step looks like:

1	Begin a workout routine	Start three times a week for 30 minutes.
2	Intensity and duration	Increase exercise to four times a week and incorporate strength training sessions.
3	Variety	Maintain four times a week consistency but diversify workouts.
4	Reinforce habits and assess changes	Achieve five times a week.

This approach ensures that your actions are not only clear but also evolve as you progress, giving room for adaptation while staying true to the ultimate vision.

STEP 4: DEDICATING DAILY EFFORT
Every significant change is the result of consistent daily efforts. By making deliberate decisions on what to do each day, you align your daily activities with your quarterly milestones and, ultimately, with your vision.
Expanding on our exercise consistency example:

◇ Q1. Effort: Every Monday, Wednesday, and Friday, dedicate 15 minutes each morning to a workout that includes stretches, push-ups, and squats. Maintain a journal to monitor progress.

◇ Q2. Effort: Extend Monday, Wednesday, and Friday workouts to 25 minutes and incorporate weights or resistance bands. Commit to a long walk or hike every Sunday.

◇ Q3. Effort: Add yoga sessions on Tuesdays and Thursdays. Persist with the established routine and conclude each day with a ten-minute evening walk.

◇ Q4. Effort: Sustain the daily routine and introduce a fitness class like dance, aerobics, or a sport every Saturday. Use the end of each week for reflection and adjustments for the forthcoming year.

Sometimes, it's helpful to visualize your progress on a calendar. Regardless of your tracking method, be open to adjust and pivot as your mind or body dictates. That's the beauty of milestones. They offer this flexibility, allowing for extra rest, or added effort when you're up for it.

You'll complete this 4-step process for each identified component to complete a well-rounded action plan for your vision statement. As you go along, you'll want to review your progress, reassess your methods, and adjust and pivot as needed. Remember, it's the everyday choices that culminate into transformative outcomes.

YOUR FINALIZED VISION BOOK (AND BOARD)

By dedicating yourself to this 4-step process annually, you'll find, in time, a completed Book of Visions, segmented by chapter and year, mapping out your life plan for the decade. As each new year approaches, be prepared to revisit the 4-step process. Grab a new notebook (or workbook templates) and:

1. Review your chapter components.
2. Frame your series of "how" questions targeting the focus area of the component.
3. Specify the actions or steps you'll take each quarter to answer the "how."
4. Plan and commit to the daily efforts aligned with the quarterly milestones.

By following this roadmap, you're not just setting intentions but laying down a clear path to actualizing your visions. With each step, you transform abstract ideas into tangible actions, turning the distant future into a reality just within reach.

As each new year approaches, the idea of creating a vision board might feel more fitting, especially with a structured path now guiding your personal journey. With confidence, attend the party, and make a board collaging your chapter components, strategies, and tactics. But as you continue to delve deeper into this journey, you'll soon realize that you possess such a profound connection to your goals and aspirations that you won't even need a physical board to serve as a reminder. Your vision will naturally manifest in your thoughts, choices, and daily actions. Embrace the process, trust in your greatness, and let each day be a step toward the new you.

chapter 10

FAITH: YOUR GREATNESS REALIZED, MANIFESTING THE UNSEEN

*T*he well-known proverb, "Seeing is believing," implies that we need tangible evidence before accepting something as real. However, the act of manifestation challenges this idea. In the world of manifestation, belief comes first. It urges us to cling to our visions and aspirations without needing immediate evidence or proof. It prompts us to trust in possibilities greater than what we see or feel, pushing boundaries and reshaping what we consider possible.

Angelina Lombardo, author of *Spiritual Entrepreneur*, captures the essence of manifestation beautifully. She says manifesting is making your desired outcomes real through your thoughts, actions, beliefs, and emotions.[7] As you dive into this chapter, I want you to know that you hold the power to manifest the outcome of every vision you've

---

7   Angelina Lombardo, *The Spiritual Entrepreneur* (Washington, DC: Difference Press, 2019).

imagined. Waiting to "see it"—if that's what causes you to "believe it"—will keep you waiting indefinitely. Instead, transform your thoughts, beliefs, and intentions by rooting them in the unshakeable confidence that your desires—all the things you are writing down in your Vision Book—are already unfolding, even if they're not yet visible.

Now that you've started writing your life's vision plan, understand the journey doesn't stop there. While we've tackled the first steps which were to plainly plan it and write it down, two more critical steps follow: believing with faith in your vision and taking decisive action toward materialization. Only with these steps undertaken will your vision truly manifest.

MANIFESTING YOUR VISION BEGINS WITH BELIEVING

To believe something is to accept it as true or real. This belief is often based on some form of evidence or reasoning. Believing is an intellectual agreement with a concept or a fact. For example, when you look at a weather app and say, "I believe it will rain tomorrow," you're relying on information presented to you. Manifestation varies in approach for everyone, but one undeniable commonality exists: you cannot manifest what you do not believe. Manifestation requires profound belief, a rock-solid assurance that your visions will come to fruition. It goes beyond mere hope; it's about firm conviction.

Bringing a vision to realization starts with a belief in the plan you've committed to paper. It's not about writing down idle wishes or far-fetched dreams; it's about recognizing your strengths, your gifts, and your Organic Brilliance as evidence of undeniable plausibility. When you write down your aspirations, it's essential to do so with the certainty that, due to who you are and the unique talents you possess, it's not just possible—it's inevitable—that they will materialize. This belief is the first critical step that sets the foundation for the vision you've planned to ultimately become a reality.

THE MANIFESTATION WAITING PERIOD

As we journey through the process of manifestation, the waiting period often emerges as the most challenging phase. You've planned and written your vision, so now what? What do you do in that span between planting the seeds and watching them bloom? What happens in the time that we're waiting for our manifestation to unfold?

While you eagerly await the manifestation of your vision, remember this—how you fill the waiting room of your desires can either reinforce the reality you seek or sabotage it entirely. What you do in this waiting period matters just as much as the effort you've put in before. This waiting time isn't a pause; it's an active period where every choice still counts. It's the time to reinforce, not undo, your hard work.

The essence of belief truly shines most during the waiting period, in the moments of anticipation. So, let's say you've written in your Vision Book that this year, you will purchase a new home. You've mapped out your plan, outlining the practical steps such as getting your finances in order, choosing the right realtor, creating a timeline, and engaging in the necessary procedures to navigate through the home-buying process. This act of writing down the vision plan is crucial—it's the blueprint laid out clearly. However, belief is the energy that animates this blueprint; it's the dynamic force working in the background while you wait for all things to fall into place.

As you await potential home listings from your realtor and gather your financial documents, you'll also need to engage yourself in planning and emotionally investing in the reality you seek to create. You see, your belief transforms the waiting period into a planning session. This is not idle daydreaming; it's strategic visualization. In your journal you begin sketching the future not in outlines but in specific declarations: the number of bedrooms, the design of the bathrooms, the ambiance of your living space. You even express gratitude and excitement for the home as if it's already yours, detailing features like a spacious master bedroom on the ground floor, and the joy you experience in decorating it. You close your eyes, you see it, and you write it down. You describe how you feel sitting on your new couch, looking out of the window of this new home. This is part of actualizing your vision—not passively hoping to see what happens but actively shaping what will be. This is not wishful thinking—it is conviction put to paper.

This practice isn't imagining; it is a demonstration of belief in fruition, underpinned by prayer and the confidence that God has sanctioned your vision. Consider how in 1 Kings 6:1-10, Solomon provides a meticulous account of the Lord's temple construction before its realization—each specification, from the cedar beams down to the carved palms and flowers, was preordained. Similarly, you can and should articulate your vision with precision, fueling your belief system. Such clarity in your prayers and intentions eliminates uncertainty. You declare it, and so, it will be.

◇◇◇◇◇◇◇◇◇◇◇◇◇◇◇◇◇◇◇◇◇◇◇◇◇◇◇◇◇◇◇◇◇

You have the power to tell your future what it looks like based on what you know God has already promised.

Understand, you have the power to tell your future what it looks like based on what you know God has already promised. It is not for you to worry over how your vision will come to pass—the mechanics are already in motion. Your role is to vividly live in the "what"—the end result. This conviction in what is not yet seen is the exercise of belief—a deep knowing that you can direct the course of your life by aligning your desires with God's will, affirming that you have agency over your destiny. It is a profound partnership with faith where you pronounce your future achievements, not as possibilities but as forthcoming chapters of your life story.

MANIFESTING YOUR FUTURE REQUIRES FAITH

When we explore our thoughts and convictions, it's crucial to differentiate between "belief" and "faith." Although they're interconnected, their nuances are significant. Remember, belief is the starting point, an acceptance of an idea because there's evidence that supports it. Faith, on the other hand, goes beyond just accepting an idea; it involves a degree of trust and reliance without the need for complete evidence. Faith is an assurance that extends beyond logic or what can be proved in the physical realm—it stems from a place of personal, spiritual, or religious conviction. Take, for instance, an entrepreneur starting a business who says, "I believe my business will succeed." This assertion isn't just based on market research or strategies; it's powered by a deep trust in their vision and hard work. Belief may ignite the spark of certainty, setting us on a path of exploration. But it is faith that sustains our journey, propelling us forward, encouraging us to act even when certainty is out of sight.

Faith, as described in Hebrews 11:1 (NIV) is the "confidence in what we hope for and assurance about what we do not see." This scripture distills faith, portraying it as a firm assurance and deep conviction in the unseen. It's an active force. Jesus underscores this in John 20:29 (NIV), saying to Thomas, "Because you have seen me, you have believed; blessed are those who have not seen and yet have believed." Here, faith is presented as a blessing—valuable and honorable—for it believes without the need for physical evidence.

In the realm of manifestation, this kind of faith is vital. It's not about passive belief but an active visualization and trust in the fruition of our desires, even before they materialize. The degree of our faith can determine the fulfillment or faltering of our visions. When we understand faith in this way—as a potent blend of trust, hope, and belief in the unseen—it becomes clear why it's a dynamic catalyst in manifesting our deepest aspirations. After all, the power of manifestation unfolds according to your faith.

THE SEEDS IN YOUR GARDEN

A thought is simply an idea that pops into your mind, either because of something you've seen or heard or from your own imagination. It's a mental note that comes and goes quite quickly. On the other hand, belief is what happens when you have the same kind of thought repeatedly until it feels like something you're sure about. It's like a thought that you keep thinking until you're convinced it's true.

Imagine your mind as a fertile garden. Each thought is like a seed in this garden, and while every seed holds the possibility to grow, it is the care we give—water, sunlight, and good soil—that truly determines whether it will sprout into life. In the same way, a single thought may come and go, but when you give it consistent attention, focus on it repeatedly, and attach strong feelings to it, that thought begins to embed itself in your consciousness, developing into a belief. You are the guardian of your mental garden. Just as a careful gardener selects which seeds to plant and tend to, you have the power to decide which thoughts to focus on and strengthen. And it is these well-tended thoughts that eventually bloom into the rooted beliefs that guide your life.

◇◇◇◇◇◇◇◇◇◇◇◇◇◇◇◇◇◇◇◇◇◇◇◇◇◇◇◇◇◇◇◇

You are the guardian of your mental garden. Just as a careful gardener selects which seeds to plant and tend to, you have the power to decide which thoughts to focus on and strengthen.

Despite a gardener's best efforts to protect their plants, they cannot prevent the forces of pollination from introducing unfamiliar seeds into their garden. The unavoidability of pollination—the transfer of seed-producing pollen from one flower to another—often happens due to external factors like wind, insects, or animals introducing foreign agents into a garden's ecosystem. Similarly, in the fertile garden of our minds, we experience a form of "mental pollination." When we encounter new information, ideas, or perspectives that drift into our consciousness, they act as intellectual grains of pollen carried into the fertile ground of our thoughts.

It is in this same way that our minds are constantly exposed to new information, ideas, and perspectives from the world around us. And just like a garden that can't fully insulate itself against the elements, our mental space is also open to infiltration from these external influences.

Despite this, it's within our power to choose which of these new thoughts we allow to germinate and integrate into our belief system. We have the choice to nurture those that align with our aspirations and to weed out those that don't. The destiny of our vision is ultimately determined by the careful selection and attentive care we give to the thoughts we cultivate. In this cultivation lies the power to shape our reality, guiding the manifestation of our vision through the thoughts we choose to turn into beliefs.

THE WEEDS IN YOUR GARDEN

Our mind is like a garden, and our thoughts are the seeds we plant in it. The choices we make in tending to this garden—what to plant and what to weed out—directly influence our actions and outcomes. This concept connects with the teachings of Proverbs 23:7 (AMP), which says, "For as he thinks in his heart, so is he [in behavior—one who manipulates]." Essentially, the ideas we allow to flourish within us, much like the seeds we carefully tend to in a garden, come to define our inner character and outward behavior. In James Allen's book *As a Man Thinketh*, he further elaborates on this biblical proverb, proposing that our character is the complete sum of our thoughts. Allen reveals the philosophical truth of the interconnectedness between our thoughts and the tangible manifestations we experience in our lives. As Allen insightfully says, "All that a man achieves and all that he fails to achieve is the direct result of his own thoughts."[8]

It excites me to think that by consciously selecting and fostering the thoughts we allow in our minds, we have the power to shape our decisions, guide our actions, and determine the eventual results of our life's journey. If we accept this principle, acknowledging that our

---

8   James Allen, *As a Man Thinketh* (Printed by Amazon, 2020) 64.

thoughts can be managed and directed, then it follows that we have a significant measure of control over the eventualities of our existence. This suggests a profound responsibility: we must cultivate our mental landscape with care and intention, understanding that from it springs the diverse outcomes of our lives.

Considering the profound impact thoughts have on directing our lives, it begs the question: How can we guide our thoughts to consistently align with our purpose, ensuring our plans envisioned manifest? What happens when we inadvertently nurture seeds of doubt, fear, or negativity, allowing them to overshadow the purpose-driven thoughts we've worked hard to cultivate? The very act of entertaining these thoughts is parallel to the weeds that sprout and spread in your meticulously cared-for garden.

Allowing doubt, fear, hesitation, and negativity to take root in your mind can overshadow the bright potential of your envisioned future. Just as rampant weeds can choke the life out of a flourishing garden, these mental adversaries can cloud your thoughts and impede your true potential. Every experienced gardener understands the necessity of vigilantly spotting and eradicating these invaders to protect the well-being of their garden. In the same way, it's critical for you to be alert and ready to counteract these harmful seeds of thought before they embed themselves and grow into disruptive weeds. Allen succinctly puts it, "Doubt and fear are the great enemies of knowledge; if you do not conquer them, they will conquer you."[9] He emphasizes that negative thoughts yield nothing productive. If neglected, they invariably lead to failure.

By cultivating constructive thoughts and weeding out the detrimental ones you create the ideal environment for possibility, positivity, and manifestation to flourish. So, remember your role as the master gardener of your mind. Embrace the responsibility to nurture thoughts that align with your highest aspirations, beliefs, and purpose. Let us embrace the wisdom

---

9   James Allen, *As a Man Thinketh*, 62.

of Proverbs 23:7, recognizing the incredible power our thoughts hold, and use it to shape a reality that reflects our esteemed levels of greatness.

THE SILENT SABOTEUR

Beliefs hold immense power, acting either as catalysts that drive us toward our goals or as weights that tether us to our current state. It's crucial to recognize that not all beliefs are rooted in fact, nor do they invariably contribute to our advancement or happiness. In fact, some beliefs can create self-fulfilling prophecies, not because they are truths in themselves but because they sculpt our actions and, therefore, shape our results. Consider, for instance, if you firmly believe that a certain goal is out of your reach, that very belief might prevent you from taking the necessary steps toward achieving it. Not because the goal was unattainable, but because it was your belief that influenced your behavior and turned the supposed impossibility into your lived experience.

◇◇◇◇◇◇◇◇◇◇◇◇◇◇◇◇◇◇◇◇◇◇◇◇◇◇◇◇◇◇◇◇◇◇

Limiting Beliefs are entrenched convictions or opinions about our identity, the world at large, and our role within it, often stemming from past experiences, societal conditioning, or negative interactions . . . restricting our potential and obscuring our vision.

I refer to these restrictive notions as "Limiting Beliefs." They function like invisible barriers, often self-imposed, that restrict our potential and dictate the perimeter of our possibilities. Limiting Beliefs are entrenched convictions or opinions about our identity, the world at large, and our role within it, often stemming from past experiences, societal conditioning, or negative interactions. These beliefs can act like a frosted glass ceiling in our minds, restricting our potential and obscuring our vision. They persuade us to accept that certain dreams are beyond our grasp and certain journeys beyond our reach. Limited Beliefs might whisper that we're not "good enough" or that success is reserved for others. They serve as the silent saboteurs of our aspirations, often more crippling than the overt doubts we recognize and combat. Identifying and confronting these hidden detractors is essential if we're to fully operate at the Pinnacle of Greatness.

THINK BIGGER. ASK BIGGER. BELIEVE BIGGER.

In Acts 3, the Bible recounts the story of a man who had been unable to walk since birth. Each day, someone would carry him to the temple gates, where he would beg for money from those entering for worship. One day, when he saw disciples Peter and John approaching, he asked them for money. Peter responded, saying he had no material possessions to offer. However, he did have something invaluable to give. Invoking the power and authority granted to him by Jesus, Peter told the man to walk. He then took the man by the hand, lifting him to his feet. Miraculously, the man's legs gained strength, and he began to walk.

This story is a powerful illustration of the interplay between faith and Limiting Belief. The man, who had been unable to walk since birth, was asking for money but not for the ability to walk. Why? Likely because the concept of walking was so far beyond what he could fathom for himself that he never dared to believe it could happen. His mindset was confined by Limiting Beliefs about his own capabilities.

On the other hand, Peter epitomizes the essence of faith. He was steadfast in his conviction that healing was possible, regardless of the circumstances. Unburdened by doubt, Peter believed in possibilities that others might deem inconceivable. On that fateful day, his faith shattered the boundaries of the lame man's Limiting Beliefs, offering him a new reality that he had never dared to dream of.

Peter shows us what faith in action looks like—operating and believing in possibilities that extend far beyond the constraints of current conditions and sometimes even mental comprehension—while the lame man exemplifies the self-imposed limitations that come from harboring restricted beliefs. Just like Peter, your faith has the transformative power to shatter any Limiting Beliefs that may be lurking deep within you. Embrace this incredible potential; your faith can illuminate possibilities you've never even dared to imagine. Let faith guide you toward a life unburdened by limitations.

OVERCOMING LIMITED BELIEFS

Overcoming limiting beliefs is a dual-step process, intertwining self-awareness with actionable change. Initially, you must identify and acknowledge that you have Limiting Beliefs. This awareness demands a thorough self-examination, prompting questions about the origin of these beliefs and their congruence with your present circumstances and vision. The next and more challenging step involves assessing the nature of your faith. It's common to hear that we need an "increase of faith"—as if it could be measured and stockpiled to guarantee greater manifestations of our desires. However, this is a misconception about the nature of faith. The quantity of faith is not what dictates our ability to transcend barriers; rather, it's about connecting even the tiniest seed of faith with conviction and purpose. It is this actionable faith, not an amount, that catalyzes change and overcomes the constraints of Limiting Beliefs.

◇◇◇◇◇◇◇◇◇◇◇◇◇◇◇◇◇◇◇◇◇◇◇◇◇◇◇◇◇◇◇◇◇◇◇◇◇

A "mustard seed" of faith, as the scripture describes, is sufficient if it's truly believed and acted upon.

According to the Bible, faith isn't a substance to be measured and expanded; it is a state of trust and conviction that, even in its smallest measure, is profoundly powerful. A "mustard seed" of faith, as the scripture describes, is sufficient if it's truly believed and acted upon. We are reminded in Matthew 17:20 (NIV) that faith the size of a mustard seed is enough to move mountains. Jesus said, "If you have faith as small as a mustard seed, you can say to this mountain, 'Move from here to there,' and it will move. Nothing will be impossible for you." This suggests that the call is not for an increase in faith but rather a strengthening of it. Even a microscopic grain of authentic faith can be transformative.

The mustard seed, one of the smallest of seeds, grows into a tree. Similarly, faith, no matter how small, signifies the presence of belief that is sufficient to connect with the power of God. It's not the scale of faith that matters but its quality and the firmness with which we hold it. Whether our faith is small or great in our eyes, it's the application of that faith—how we live it out in our thoughts, words, and actions—that truly makes the difference in our lives.

DOUBT: THE KILLER OF FAITH

Doubt can be the greatest destructor of faith. While faith is about belief and trust, even in the unseen or unknown, doubt acts as a weed in the garden of belief. It starts small, but if allowed to grow, it can overwhelm and weaken the very foundations of your faith. The moment doubt creeps in, it challenges and erodes the certainty that faith upholds. Therefore, it's crucial to recognize and address doubts as they arise, ensuring they don't take root and diminish the strength and resilience of your faith. Just as a gardener diligently removes weeds to protect their garden, so must we tend to our inner garden of faith, keeping it free from the invasive growth of doubt.

In the book of Matthew, we encounter a significant story of a woman seeking deliverance for her daughter. In the story, Jesus acknowledges the woman's great faith. However, this description of "great" faith is often misunderstood as a larger quantity of faith. But my take is that it wasn't necessarily the size of her faith but the absence of doubt that made her faith great. In Matthew 15:28 (NKJV), Jesus tells the Canaanite woman, "O woman, great is your faith! Let it be to you as you desire." It was her display of unwavering belief—without a hint of skepticism or doubt—in Jesus's power to heal and deliver. Her faith was great not because of its volume but because it was pure and unadulterated by doubt. Therefore, when confronting your Limiting Beliefs, it's not about praying for an increase of faith but rather nurturing that mustard seed faith within us, ensuring that it's undiluted by doubt, in line with your perspective.

If you discover that your faith is weakened because of doubt, or you're struggling to fully believe in the potential you've envisioned, consider praying for less doubt to strengthen your mustard seed faith. Let your faith be fortified by remembering my favorite faith-activator scriptures, Philippians 4:13 (NIV): "I can do all things through Him who gives me strength." And Jesus's words in Matthew that with faith, nothing will be impossible for you. Remember, your faith has the power to destroy your Limiting Beliefs, paving the way for limitless possibilities.

PLANNING AND FAITH: CHARTING THE COURSE FOR MANIFESTATION

As you think about these last two chapters, a journal can be an invaluable tool in this process to write down your blessings and all the details of what's to come. This will help to fuel your beliefs and strengthen your faith. This will also sharpen your focus, help you foster a mindset of abundance, and refine your vision with specificity and clarity. With your vision as your compass, revisit the teachings of faith in this chapter and anchor yourself in the belief that what you seek is already on its way to you. Remember, it's your faith that propels you into the realm of possibility and action.

◇◇◇◇◇◇◇◇◇◇◇◇◇◇◇◇◇◇◇◇◇◇◇◇◇◇◇◇◇◇◇◇◇

Where a Limiting Belief might whisper, "I am not worthy," overwrite it with the resounding truth, "I am deserving and capable."

186 *at the pinnacle of* GREATNESS

Also, be sure to confront the shackles of Limiting Beliefs that threaten to keep you latched to mediocrity. In your journal, document your self-imposed doubts and then begin to systematically dismantle them. Where a Limiting Belief might whisper, "I am not worthy," overwrite it with the resounding truth, "I am deserving and capable." Let this act of rewriting be a declaration of your potential and your commitment to rise above.

In the next chapter, we will conclude this section by unveiling the final steps to bring the full maturation of your vision into light. Don't think of this as the conclusion of a process but the beginning of a lifelong practice of creation and manifestation. Let's move forward with hearts ready to receive and hands prepared to shape the future we envision.

chapter 11

ACTION: YOUR GREATNESS REQUIRES LIVING WITH THE END IN MIND

In the childhood story *The Little Engine That Could*, a small blue engine, armed with determination and a belief in possibility, took on a challenge that others believed too difficult. In the story, there was a long train of cars stranded on the wrong side of a mountain, and for various reasons, several larger engines refused to help the stranded train. But the small blue engine, despite never having done such a task and being uncertain of her capabilities, decided to try.

As the Little Engine started her journey, she repeatedly chanted, "I think I can," fueling her drive. But as she climbed, a deeper conviction took hold. It was no longer a mere "thought" that she could do it that mattered but, instead, a solid belief in herself. Her position of "I think I can" changed to a declaration of "I know I can." Empowered by her belief, she put her faith into motion and achieved her mission.

Similarly, in our journey of manifestation, it's paramount to combine our faith with decisive action.

The story vividly illustrates how a well-defined plan, combined with unwavering faith, can pave the way to triumph. Here's how:

Plan: From the start, the little engine was clear on her objective: to reach the top and rescue the stranded train. She wasn't vague or uncertain; her mission was well-defined.

Faith: Initially, the little engine expressed her intention as a possibility by repeating, "I think I can." But she transformed her thoughts into a budding belief. As she continued her tough climb, her faith deepened. That once tentative whisper of "I think I can" evolved into a resounding, "I know I can." This was her transition from hope to firm faith.

However, it also hints at a crucial element we've yet to explore—action.

Action: The little engine's plan and faith would have been in vain had she not paired them with action. Simply believing she could climb the hill wouldn't move her an inch forward. It was her relentless drive, chug by chug, the steady effort despite the odds, that made her climb and eventual success possible.

The little engine's journey beautifully exemplifies the manifestation process. It reminds us that knowing what we want is just the beginning. Transforming our desires into faith sets the foundation. But, to bring our vision to life, just as the little engine did, the third step requires dedicated action.

◇◇◇◇◇◇◇◇◇◇◇◇◇◇◇◇◇◇◇◇◇◇◇◇◇◇◇◇◇◇◇◇

Planning + Faith + Action = Manifestation

PLANNING + FAITH + ACTION = MANIFESTATION

So far, we've outlined two of the three critical steps necessary for manifestation. First, we delved into the significance of having a plan around your vision and the importance of writing it down plainly. Next, we emphasized the transformative power of believing with unwavering faith in that plan for our vision. But, as the tale of the little engine reminds us, there's a crucial third component: taking decisive action toward materialization.

In the book of James, the Bible distinctly illustrates the intimate connection between faith and action:

> What good is it, my brothers and sisters, if someone claims
> to have faith but has no deeds? Can such faith save them?
> Suppose a brother or a sister is without clothes and daily
> food. If one of you says to them, "Go in peace; keep warm
> and well fed," but does nothing about their physical needs,
> what good is it? In the same way, faith by itself, if it is not
> accompanied by action, is dead. —James 2:14-17 (NIV)

This scripture reminds us that faith, as powerful as it may be, remains incomplete without tangible action. It's one thing to acknowledge our beliefs or to hold a vision; it's another to actively work toward making it a reality. James uses the example of how seeing someone in need and simply offering kind words without the actual act of helping results in no change. Similarly, holding a vision without action leaves it unfulfilled. Our faith demands evidence through our actions. Like the engine's efforts up the hill, our words and actions, grounded in faith and a clear plan, bridge the gap between our visions and their real-world manifestations.

THE POWER OF WORDS

Understanding the power of words is essential when acting toward the manifestation of a vision. The words we express are not just sounds into the atmosphere—they are declarations of our faith, serving as catalysts that propel us into corresponding action. There exists a dynamic interplay where belief gives rise to words, words strengthen your faith, and faith ignites action. Together, they form a unified force that drives us toward realizing our visions. The harmony between what we believe, say, and do is indispensable. It's this alignment that steers us toward turning our envisioned future into tangible reality.

◇◇◇◇◇◇◇◇◇◇◇◇◇◇◇◇◇◇◇◇◇◇◇◇◇◇◇◇◇◇◇◇◇◇◇◇

The harmony between what we believe, say, and do is indispensable. It's this alignment that steers us toward turning our envisioned future into tangible reality.

Your words have a direct impact on your faith and the reality you create. They can breathe life into your vision and solidify your beliefs, steering your life in a chosen direction. The Bible speaks to the significance of our speech in Proverbs 18:20-21 (AMP):

A man's stomach will be satisfied with the fruit of his mouth; He will be satisfied with the consequence of his words. Death and life are in the power of the tongue, And those who love it and indulge it will eat its fruit and bear the consequences of their words.

This scripture underscores the incredible power of speech—our words can either unlock great potential or unleash harmful effects. It is essential to recognize and respect this power, shaping our words to foster growth and positivity.

The concept of "death" in this context refers to the detrimental outcomes that stem from negative, careless, or harmful words. This isn't limited to external communication; it includes the often overlooked but equally potent internal self-talk. Regular negative self-talk can chip away at our confidence and limit our potential. Conversely, "life" represents the constructive outcomes that arise from positive affirmations and encouraging dialogue. It's about using our words to verbalize our dreams, to share kindness, and to assert our goals with conviction. By doing so, we tap into the life-giving aspect of our words, channeling our speech as a tool for manifesting the best in our lives and the lives of others.

I recall an experience from the early days of dating my husband, highlighting for me the immense, and often subconscious, power our words possess. Whenever I would share plans or discuss potential activities, he often responded with an air of pessimism. For instance, let's say I casually mentioned wanting to visit the mall in the afternoon. His instinctive response might be, "Well, you better hope it doesn't rain." It struck me because the possibility of rain wasn't even on my radar; the skies were clear, and no forecast had hinted at a downpour. Yet, his first reaction was to envision a negative outcome—one that, if realized, would put a damper on my plans. When I pointed this out to him, he expressed genuine surprise. He hadn't been consciously trying to be negative; it was just a habitual response. But therein lies the lesson: The death inherent in our tongue's power doesn't necessarily stem from intentional negativity. It can be the product of unchecked habits or subconscious beliefs.

DECREE A THING

Words aren't just arbitrary sounds; the tongue's power isn't just in what we express but also in what we declare. When we declare something with intention and conviction, we're not just speaking; we're setting the universe in motion to align with our statement. The verse from Job 22:28 (NKJV) underlines this potent principle, suggesting that our declarations can become self-fulfilling prophecies. It states, "You will also declare a thing, And it will be established for you." This scripture highlights the profound impact of our verbal declarations.

◇◇◇◇◇◇◇◇◇◇◇◇◇◇◇◇◇◇◇◇◇◇◇◇◇◇◇◇◇◇◇◇◇

When we declare something with intention and conviction, we're not just speaking; we're setting the universe in motion to align with our statement

When you speak something into existence with confidence, aligning it with your faith and purpose, it holds immense power. It's as though our words lay down the tracks for the train of our life to follow. When we align what we declare with our faith and purpose, we create a synergy that lights the path ahead. This is an active, faith-driven proclamation that sets the foundations for our aspirations to materialize. As we speak with certainty and faith, we're not just forecasting the future; we're actively participating in its construction.

Understanding the weight and impact of our words is critical in navigating life with intention. Words are more than a communication tool; they are the architects of our reality. They echo our beliefs, frame our perceptions, and instrumentally shape our destinies. By speaking with deliberate intent and clear vision, our words become powerful affirmations, guiding us toward the life we aim to create. As you continue the path of self-discovery and purpose, let your words guide, affirm, and reflect the profound life you've imagined for your future.

TAKE ACTION: LIVE WITH THE END IN MIND

To truly manifest something, you have to live like it's already done, like you've already achieved it. This isn't just wishful thinking—it's a mindset. Every part of you, from how you present yourself, to the thoughts that swirl in your head, to the words that you speak, should resonate with your intended outcome. It's these everyday actions and choices that strengthen and validate the faith you're placing in your vision.

Consider these nine lifestyle actions designed precisely for this purpose—to help reinforce and guide you in living this way:

ACTION 1: PROMISE—STAND ON HIS PROMISES

Have you ever attended a church service where the pastor encouraged the congregation to "Praise Him like it's already done?" This speaks to the idea of operating with the conviction that because you've sought God for guidance and blessings, your desires will materialize because of His promises. Numbers 23:19 reinforces this by reminding us that God is not a man that He should lie; if He has spoken it, He will indeed fulfill it. As for our requests and the desires of our hearts, John 14:14 affirms that if we ask anything in His name, He will do it, and Ephesians 4:20 emphasizes the abundance that comes through Him. The action here is simple yet profound: live as if your request has already been fulfilled. Embrace that reality now. If you truly believe in His Word, then there's no reason for you to live any differently.

The Bible is more than just a guide for spiritual living; it's a source of divine promises designed to sustain you. Engage with it—read it, study it. It is the living Word, capable of providing exactly what you need, exactly when you need it. It reaffirms God's promises, reminding us that we are not destined for constant struggle but for a life of abundance and divine purpose. It also equips us with the power to stand on those promises until we see our visions fully manifest.

ACTION 2: PRESENTATION—LIVE YOUR BELIEF OUT LOUD

How we present ourselves, our actions, and our behaviors often mirrors our internal beliefs and convictions. As you're on this journey to manifest a particular vision, it's essential that your mannerisms, actions, and even your daily routines align with that vision.

For example, let's imagine Cristina, a high school senior who has a vision to be a renowned motivational speaker and author. She's clarified her vision and believes in her heart that her words can inspire change. She's even taking public speaking and writing class electives and plans to earn a college degree in journalism and communication. But while she's waiting to complete her classes and earn her degree, she begins living and presenting herself as if she's already achieved her dream.

At social gatherings, Cristina discusses her passions, shares uplifting stories, and offers words of encouragement. On social media, she doesn't just repost others' quotes; she writes her own, sharing her ideas and insights. She offers messages on topics close to her heart to motivate and inspire others. Her friends even noticed the shift and say things like, "Cristina, you always have such a positive outlook," or "Your words really touched me." When people meet her, they feel the energy of a motivational speaker, even though she has yet to stand on a global stage or write a bestselling book.

Cristina is living her vision daily, and people can see it. They don't see someone "trying" to be a motivational speaker; they see a motivational speaker in the making. But imagine if Cristina consistently shared negative opinions on social media and habitually complained about every obstacle she encountered to anyone who would listen. Those around her would undoubtedly question whether her aspirations were even achievable, given the stark contrast in her behavior. So, it's fundamental to remember: people should be able to see the progress and milestones of your vision in your day-to-day actions over time. It's not just about the end goal but living each day congruently with that goal. The harmony between your internal convictions and your external presentation will not only inspire others but will continually affirm and reinforce your journey toward manifestation.

ACTION 3: PURPOSE—REMEMBER YOUR "WHY" AND YOUR "WHO"

During the journey toward manifestation, it's easy to become so focused on our own aspirations that we might forget the broader picture. It's crucial to remind yourself that this journey is not just about you; it's about a greater calling. Each vision, each goal, is tied to a purpose larger than you. It's not just about the desires you hold close to your heart; it's about the lives that will change because of them.

Hebrews 13:16 (NIV) reminds us, "And do not forget to do good and to share with others, for with such sacrifices God is pleased." This verse assures us of the divine calling we all have: it's not just about achieving personal success but about connecting that success to outcomes that benefit others. Your distinctive talents and journeys are crafted not merely for your own growth but to uplift and inspire those around you.

There are individuals out there who will find solace, strength, and hope through your story. They are drawn to you, awaiting the lessons only you can teach. So, while you're waiting for your vision to come to fruition, remember that your story's power isn't just for you. The resilience you showcase, the grace with which you handle setbacks, will serve as a guiding light for others. Keep that larger purpose in mind, as it will not only sustain you while waiting but will also enrich the lives of those you're destined to touch.

ACTION 4: PREPARATION—LIVE IN ANTICIPATION OF WHAT WILL BE

It's commonly said and rooted in scripture (1 Corinthians 10:13) that God will not give us more than we can bear. Often, we think of this scripture in the context of enduring hardships, believing that if a challenge comes our way, God knows we have the strength to overcome it. But have you ever considered this concept in both directions? Not just in terms of trials and tribulations but in terms of blessings and responsibilities?

While the scripture suggests that God won't burden us with challenges we can't handle, it also implies that certain blessings might not come our way if we're not ready to handle them responsibly. It's a matter of trust. If we demonstrate that we can't wisely manage what we currently have, how can He entrust us with more? Think of it in financial terms. If you're reckless with $1,000, spending without thought or plan, why would He bless you with $100,000? The larger amount would only amplify the problems of poor financial management.

This action of preparation is about aligning your present behaviors with the future you desire. Prepare now for the lifestyle you're seeking to manifest. If you want to be trusted with bigger blessings, show you're responsible with the smaller ones because if you can't handle the small, He may not give you the large. So, prepare yourself by aligning your life with the greater blessings you aim to manifest. Preparation isn't just about readiness; it's about demonstrating trustworthiness.

ACTION 5: PURGE—RELEASE, FORGIVE, AND HEAL

Ephesians 4:31-32 (NIV) instructs:

Get rid of all bitterness, rage, and anger, brawling, and slander, along with every form of malice. Be kind and compassionate to one another, forgiving each other, just as in Christ God forgave you.

This scripture powerfully communicates that forgiveness is not just a divine command; it's a pathway to personal transformation. Unforgiveness, bitterness, and unresolved anger are chains that hold us back, preventing us from fully embracing the promises God has for us. These negative feelings don't just hinder our spiritual walk; they also impact our mental and emotional well-being. By clinging to past hurts, we are the ones who suffer the most. Holding onto these negative emotions serves as a weight that keeps us tied to the past and hinders our forward progression.

As we aspire for greater things in our lives and seek to manifest our visions, we must take an honest look inward. Ask yourself, what do you need to clean up, release, or heal from that's hurting you? Could it be that the very obstacle standing in your way is something you have control over, like unforgiveness? Releasing and forgiving is an active process that leads to healing. Moving past the hurt will clear the way for your visions to fully manifest.

ACTION 6: PRAYER—TALK TO GOD AND LISTEN TOO

Prayer is an action that ensures your vision is in alignment with God's grand design for you. When you pray, you open a direct channel of communication with the One who can guide you from where you are to where you need to be. He helps you refine your vision, revealing not only what you need to do but what you need to avoid, the distractions you need to set aside, and the lessons you need to learn along the way.

Prayer is more than a monologue; it's a dialogue. It's not just an opportunity for you to talk to God; it's also an occasion to listen for His guidance, wisdom, and reassurance. The Bible is filled with verses that emphasize the power of prayer, but the one that stands out for me is 1 John 5:14-15 (NIV):

This is the confidence we have in approaching God: that if we ask anything according to his will, he hears us. And if we know that he hears us—whatever we ask—we know that we have what we asked of him.

This scripture emphasizes why it's essential to align our visions with God's will. When you pray in alignment with His will, you're not just hoping for manifestation; you're promised it.

ACTION 7: PATIENCE—UNDERSTAND, GOOD THINGS TAKE TIME

In a world obsessed with instant gratification, patience can often feel like a forgotten art. Yet, a pillar of love is patience, and loving yourself means having the patience to allow your vision to unfold naturally, at its own pace. Just like that pot roast that has been marinated overnight and slow-cooked to perfection, good things take time. It's easy to feel pressured by the rapid-paced world around us, where achievements are showcased daily, and success stories seemingly sprout overnight. But if we rush our journey, we might miss the lessons, experiences, and growth that come with time. Remember, waiting is not wasted time; it's an active process of ensuring that what manifests is not just good but great—sustainable and not just instantaneous.

◇◇◇◇◇◇◇◇◇◇◇◇◇◇◇◇◇◇◇◇◇◇◇◇◇◇◇◇◇◇◇

Remember, waiting is not wasted time; it's an active process of ensuring that what manifests is not just good but great— sustainable and not just instantaneous.

Waiting actively ensures you don't settle for the temporary but, instead, hold out for what has been seasoned, refined, and prepared just for you. Learn to be patient with yourself, knowing that your vision is marinating, slow-cooking, and ultimately will be worth every moment you spend in faithful anticipation. The "action" in waiting is not passive; it's a conscious choice to grow, learn, and prepare for the manifestation of your vision.

ACTION 8: PROPHECY—SHAPE YOUR WORLD WITH WORDS

Prophetic, by its very nature, means foretelling or predicting the future using divine inspiration. When we use this term in the context of personal development and faith, it often implies the act of "speaking into existence" words to dictate an outcome of what we believe will happen in our lives. This is a deeply empowering action, offering you control over the narrative of your life.

Words possess an intrinsic power, either to create or to destroy. When you declare positive, affirming statements, when you speak your visions into the world, you are, in essence, prophetically directing your paths. However, the reverse is also true. Negativity and doubt also have their own prophetic weight. Statements like "I can't" or "It's impossible" don't just reflect your current state of mind; they also act as blueprints for your future.

It's not just our words that have this prophetic influence; the words of others can also prophetically release disruption by swaying our belief systems. Those voices that whisper discouragement, saying things like, "Just give up" or "You're never going to be able to do that," are also prophesying over your life. Their words can act as gateways, allowing fear and doubt to seep into your consciousness. It's critical to remember that every spoken word has energy and intention behind it that can shape and alter the path of our journey. By understanding and practicing the action of prophecy, you're not merely hoping for the best. You're declaring it, shaping it, and inviting it into your life. Like a sculptor who starts with a block of marble, your words chip away at the excess, gradually revealing the masterpiece that is your vision. So speak wisely, speak purposefully, and speak positively. Your future is listening.

ACTION 9: PERSPECTIVE—FIND OPPORTUNITY IN EVERY OUTCOME

Perspective isn't just about how you view situations; it's about understanding that every twist and turn, every delay and detour, serves a higher purpose in your journey toward manifestation. With the right mindset, nothing is a setback; everything is a lesson, a shield, or a catalyst driving you closer to your vision. For instance, if you're on your way to an important event and your flight gets delayed, a basic outlook might lead to frustration because of the disruption in plans. But an empowered perspective, grounded in the principles of manifestation, prompts you to see the delay as an opportunity—a chance to regroup, strategize, or even take a moment for self-care.

The scripture, Romans 8:28 (NIV), tells us how to view instances of life: "And we know that in all things God works for the good of those who love him, who have been called according to his purpose." Operating in His purpose for us assures that, even in the face of setbacks or frustrations, God orchestrates everything for our benefit. So, when life takes an unexpected turn, the action of shifting your perspective is twofold: Firstly, it constantly reaffirms your understanding that life's events are always steering you toward your vision and purpose. Secondly, when faced with what seems like an obstacle, pause, reflect, and pivot your perspective to see the hidden opportunity. Allow this active mindset to propel you, knowing that each event, however seemingly insignificant or disruptive, is a stepping stone toward manifestation.

These nine actions are your keys to manifestation. Respect them as essential practices, each one fine-tuning your alignment with the destiny that awaits you.

A PRAYER FOR BRIDGING VISION AND REALITY

Dear Lord,

Grant me the strength and wisdom to actively pursue the vision You've planted within my heart. Guide my steps as I endeavor to turn my plans into reality, providing me with the resolve to act diligently and intentionally each day. May I remain alert to Your divine direction, embracing every opportunity and challenge as a chance to grow closer to the future You've designed for me.

Help me to celebrate each achievement, however small, and learn from the setbacks without losing heart. Infuse me with the courage to make necessary adjustments, understanding that the path You've set before me may require flexibility and resilience. As I walk this journey, keep me strengthened in my faith, trusting that You are with me, fortifying my spirit, and leading me to manifest Your purpose for my life.

In every moment of doubt or uncertainty, remind me that with You, all things are possible. Encourage me to not just dream but to act, for it is through my actions that I honor Your will and draw closer to the reality You've promised. May my every effort reflect my commitment to Your plan, bridging the gap between my present and my envisioned future for Your glory. Amen.

section 4

STRATEGY

chapter 12

DNA: YOUR GREATNESS IS UNCLONABLE

Every individual carries within them a blueprint as distinct and intricate as their very existence—this is the marvel of DNA. Deoxyribonucleic acid, or DNA, is not just a scientific term; it is the fundamental code that crafts the singularity of who we are. Like an artist's signature on a masterpiece, DNA is our body's unique mark of identity, a molecular fingerprint that is irreplicable.

Despite the shared traits within families or even the near-mirrored genetics of identical twins, each person's DNA has variations that set them apart. It's a natural phenomenon that ensures that even in the minute differences, no two individuals are perfectly identical. Your DNA does more than just determine the color of your eyes or the shape of your nose; it's an intimate journal of your ancestral heritage, a story told in billions of genetic letters. Consider the way DNA comes into play in forensics, where just a few cells left at a scene can reveal the identity of a person. It's evidence of how definitive and exclusive our DNA is. In that same vein, your life, your experiences, and the stories

206 *at the pinnacle of* GREATNESS

you share carry the same level of unparalleled authenticity. They are yours alone, a collection of moments that no one else can claim or copy.

◇◇◇◇◇◇◇◇◇◇◇◇◇◇◇◇◇◇◇◇◇◇◇◇◇◇◇◇◇◇◇◇◇◇◇

As you navigate through your unique existence, remember that your Greatness is as unclonable as the DNA that resides within every cell of your being.

In understanding the exclusivity of our DNA, we find a metaphor for our own lives. Just as no two strands of DNA are identical, no two paths in life are the same. Your journey, with its victories, struggles, and lessons, is yours to live and yours to share. The stories you tell—the trials you've endured and triumphed over—serve as motivation and courage for others. As you navigate through your unique existence, remember that your Greatness is as unclonable as the DNA that resides within every cell of your being. Embrace the unparalleled narrative you're living, for it holds the power to inspire and uplift, to teach and to comfort. It's a testament to the fact that there is, indeed, no one else quite like you.

NAVIGATING THE PATH TO VISIBILITY: YOUR UNIQUE STRATEGY

Your journey is more than personal growth; it's about developing a strategy to connect with those who need the wisdom and strength you've gained. Your strategy is about transforming your life experiences into a relatable and engaging story, one that resonates with people facing obstacles you've already conquered. Your experiences, the challenges you've overcome, and the victories you've celebrated are not just personal triumphs—they're invaluable lessons for others.

The effectiveness of your strategy lies in how you share these experiences to make a meaningful impact. It's about taking the highs and lows of your life and presenting them in a way that offers hope and guidance. Think of your strategy as your method of broadcasting a signal to the right audience. This isn't about broad exposure; it's about forging genuine, impactful relationships. It's about aligning every aspect of your outreach with the core of your experiences and the lessons they hold. This alignment not only attracts those who are meant to find inspiration and guidance from you but also helps you evolve into the best version of yourself.

Your strategy is a vital connector between your personal journey and your greater purpose. It acts as the guide for your actions, ensuring each step is not just in line with your vision but also presenting your identity and purpose in a way that resonates with and uplifts others, propelling you toward the life you're meant to live.

A LIFE LESSON FROM BRUCE LEE

Bruce Lee, renowned as a groundbreaking martial artist, also left an enduring legacy of philosophical wisdom. His purpose transcends beyond the realm of combat, offering universal insights into self-expression, personal freedom, and the essence of life itself. He once said the following:

> *When I look around, I always learn something, and that is to always be yourself, and to express yourself, to have faith in yourself. Do not go out and look for a successful personality*

and duplicate it. Start from the very root of your being, which is "how can I be me?"[10]

Drawing inspiration from Bruce Lee, we realize the power of individuality and the importance of authenticity. Life doesn't stop at identifying a vision and living toward its manifestation. While your vision outlines your ultimate goals and the milestones to achieve them, your strategy delves into the narrative behind those achievements. For example, let's say you have a desire to live a life maintaining a healthy weight. Your vision might outline the specific weight goals, exercise regimens, and dietary plans you intend to follow. It would provide a clear endpoint and the stepping stones to reach it.

However, the strategy embodies the journey—the challenges faced, the emotional highs and lows, the insights gained, and the transformative experiences that made the vision a reality. It's the story you share with others, turning your personal journey into a relatable, inspiring guide for those facing similar struggles. The strategy provides a framework not just for achieving a goal but for narrating the unique, unclonable journey you took to get there.

Just as Bruce Lee encourages us to embrace our individuality, your strategy introduces ways to brand it by crafting a business to share your unique story. It's about packaging your journey into a program or product tailored for your specific audience. Your strategy is essentially your business plan but for marketing the distinguished brand that is you. It's about designing a well-organized process to showcase your life journey to the world and connect with those who resonate with your purpose. A properly executed strategy becomes your legacy—a life story of impact that outlives your lifespan.

---

10 Bruce Lee, "The Philosophies," *Bruce Lee*, www.brucelee.com/philosophies.

YOUR JOURNEY IS INCOMPARABLE

Steve Jobs once said, "Your time is limited, don't waste it living someone else's life."[11] Admiring someone is one thing but trying to replicate their journey? That's a different story. Each person's path is unique and unclonable. We aren't meant to be mere copies of others. While drawing inspiration from someone is constructive, becoming fascinated with mirroring their life as an attempt to achieve the same outcome is not. The results of your life, along with the unique blueprint of how you achieved them, are distinctly yours and can't be duplicated.

◇◇◇◇◇◇◇◇◇◇◇◇◇◇◇◇◇◇◇◇◇◇◇◇◇◇◇◇◇

Your life's journey is unparalleled and becomes your story to tell. Even if the goals you set align with those of others, the route you take to achieve them will be distinctly yours.

Your life's journey is unparalleled and becomes your story to tell. Even if the goals you set align with those of others, the route you take to achieve them will be distinctly yours. This is why your story is important. Recognizing that your unique "how" can't be copied allows you to fully embrace your journey, accepting the ups and downs that lead you to your destiny. Even if people attempt to impersonate you, they will never be you because it's your shared, personally lived experiences that make you relatable and affectionately genuine.

---

11 Antonia Sterian, "Steve Jobs–A Tangled Set of Circumstances," *StartUs Magazine*, 15 June 2017, magazine.startus.cc/steve-jobs-tangled-set-circumstances/.

Adopting an unclonable strategy involves cherishing every part of yourself and recognizing that your path has been intentionally orchestrated for you. So, let go of the aspects of yourself that might have once caused embarrassment; let them become sources to embrace. What you may have felt ashamed of, learn to accept. The comparisons you've made to others will reveal themselves as reflections of your own internal competition. So, rather than harboring resentment or displeasure for what you lack, cultivate gratitude for being entrusted with the responsibility to achieve more with less.

GOD USES ORDINARY PEOPLE FOR EXTRAORDINARY ASSIGNMENTS

God employs ordinary individuals to fulfill extraordinary missions. Moses, despite his impeded speech, led hundreds out of captivity (Exodus 4). David, not renowned for his stature, overcame a giant with a mere stone and slingshot (1 Samuel 17). Esther, an orphan without family, rose to become a queen who ruled over those who had once persecuted her lineage (Book of Esther). Hannah, once barren and subjected to ridicule, gave birth to a son, Samuel, in her later years, who was a significant prophet and judge in Israel (1 Samuel 1-2). Each instance illustrates how God uses imperfect people for a greater purpose. So why do we believe we must be perfect or have it all together for Him to use us for His plan?

The story of King Saul is a powerful example of how God uses imperfect people to fulfill His plans. Saul, who was initially searching for lost donkeys, unexpectedly found himself on a path set by divine design. After failing to find the donkeys, Saul's servant suggested they seek advice from Samuel, a prophet known for his great insights. Before

Saul could ask about the donkeys, Samuel reassured him they were safe and unexpectedly invited him to a feast with the priests.

Saul, who considered himself insignificant, being from Israel's smallest tribe, the Benjamites, was taken aback by Samuel's hospitality. He expressed his disbelief and humility in 1 Samuel 9:21, questioning why he was being treated with such importance. Despite his reservations, Samuel led Saul to dine, seating him at the head of the table, and offering him a portion of meat reserved for honored guests.

As the story unfolds, Samuel reveals God's plan to anoint Saul as king. Struggling with feelings of inadequacy and unworthiness because of where he was from, Saul could not understand why he was singled out for such a prestigious honor. Becoming king was neither a desire nor a prayer of Saul's, yet he was chosen by God. This story highlights a key theme: God often selects humble and seemingly ordinary people for extraordinary roles.

Saul's initial struggle mirrors what we identify today as imposter syndrome, a psychological pattern where a person has the belief of being unqualified or undeserving of a position or assignment. When you find yourself chosen by God for a task you feel unprepared for, take comfort and stand confident in knowing that He will equip and guide you through it. When Saul expresses his doubt to Samuel, he comforts Saul, reassuring him that since God has chosen him, He will mold him into the person needed for the assignment (1 Samuel 10:6). Samuel emphasizes that Saul need not worry, as God's presence and guidance will be with him.

There's a quote by Marshall Thurber that I constantly reference as my weed killer when I feel a level of inadequacy creeping in. It says, "God does not give a lick of an ice cream cone without wanting you to have the whole cone." If God gives you an idea or assigns you a task, He has every intention of guiding you, providing for you, and ensuring that you can see it through to completion. This quote serves as a reassurance for me that with every vision, assignment, or idea that originates from God, He will also provide the means, guidance, and resources necessary for me to deliver. God doesn't just give partially; if He provides a glimpse of favor or blessing, it's a sign that He intends to provide fully and abundantly. Your obedience rewards you with the grace to succeed because greater is He that is in you. And it's His working within you that sparks miraculous outcomes and life-changing results. In other words, God always wants you to enjoy the whole ice cream cone.

◇◇◇◇◇◇◇◇◇◇◇◇◇◇◇◇◇◇◇◇◇◇◇◇◇◇◇◇◇◇◇◇◇

With every vision, assignment, or idea that originates from God, He will also provide the means, guidance, and resources necessary for me to deliver.

When you attain success purely through God's guidance and blessings, your life unfolds into a story that captivates and inspires. This was evident in Saul's journey; as people witnessed the transformative power of God within him, they were astounded, asking, "Is this the same Saul, the son of Kish?" By embracing our distinctive identity and fearlessly chasing our divine purpose, we will naturally pique others' curiosity. The more unconventional your story, the more it repels replication and the more fascinating it becomes to others. And within that intrigue lies a golden opportunity: not just to share your story but also to testify about God's hand in it. This also serves as an indirect invitation for others to explore what it might be like to allow God to navigate their journeys as well.

It's important to discover the unclonable aspects of yourself—even those you might have concealed out of discomfort or shame. What about your story is unusual? What might you have been previously embarrassed about makes your story far more intriguing because of that factor? Integrate these elements into your strategy, demonstrating to others how even the unconventional can accomplish the unimaginable.

A LESSON FROM A MATH TEACHER

Navigating spaces where others deem you unworthy (even when God qualifies you) will inevitably invite scrutiny, even as you faithfully serve those to whom you are called. But know this: You weren't made to gain the world's approval. You were not created to be loved by the world. Despite your good deeds, be prepared for critics to highlight any perceived flaws.

◇◇◇◇◇◇◇◇◇◇◇◇◇◇◇◇◇◇◇◇◇◇◇◇◇◇◇◇◇◇◇◇

Despite your good deeds, be prepared for critics to highlight any perceived flaws.

One day, as I was browsing through LinkedIn, I stumbled upon a powerful video that depicted, in mere minutes, the essence of the world's perception and behavior. In the video, there was a math teacher writing on a board the multipliers of the number nine. With precision, he wrote 9x1=9, 9x2=18, and so on, until he made an intentional mistake at 9x10, which he displayed as 91. The classroom roared with laughter, a student even mocking, "Good one." Capitalizing on this moment, the teacher confessed the error was deliberate to teach a vital lesson.

He begins explaining how the class witnessed him writing the correct equation nine times, but no one applauded him for that. But as soon as he made a mistake, they all laughed and criticized him. He emphasized that while nine correct answers didn't elicit a response, one error was immediately called out. Through this exercise, he highlighted society's tendency to criticize quickly and to praise and find the positive much more slowly. He cautioned his students that they, too, would face criticism many times in their lives. And those who are lucky enough to become "successful" will likely experience more criticism than the rest. He highlighted a harsh reality: you'll find that one thing people love more than pointing out others' mistakes is when they can do it to someone who's achieved more than them. Yet, such criticism often reveals the critic's own insecurities because those who are happy with themselves rarely feel compelled to point out the faults in others.

Here are key pieces of wisdom I gathered from this video about navigating criticism, especially as you work to achieve success:

◇ Embrace feedback from those who challenge you constructively.
◇ Always strive to see the best intentions of others.
◇ Instead of highlighting errors, kindly offer corrections and ensure your compliments outnumber your criticisms.
◇ Growth happens in environments of support and constructive criticism, not in echo chambers of agreement.
◇ Distinguish between criticism that helps you grow and negativity that doesn't serve you.

◇ Your journey is about your progress—not pleasing everyone.
◇ Understand your strengths and remember your potential.
◇ If you're being criticized, you're likely making moves and giving people something to talk about.
◇ See criticism as a marker of your involvement and impact in the world.
◇ Every great achievement was once doubted. Keep moving forward.

In a world that often magnifies missteps and minimizes victories, maintaining your self-worth amidst the criticism is crucial. The teacher's insightful lesson rings true: achievements often get whispered while criticism gets amplified. We are in a world that is quick to judge and slow to understand. Navigate through life knowing that criticism is often a reflection of the critic's own insecurities, not your worth or abilities. As you elevate in your journey, remember: the taller the tree, the stronger the wind it faces. So, stand tall, stay grounded, and let the winds of criticism only strengthen your roots.

◇◇◇◇◇◇◇◇◇◇◇◇◇◇◇◇◇◇◇◇◇◇◇◇◇◇◇◇◇◇◇

The taller the tree, the stronger the wind it faces. So, stand tall, stay grounded, and let the winds of criticism only strengthen your roots.

DON'T EXPECT THE WORLD TO LOVE YOU

Understand, there are people who gain satisfaction from your misfortune, eager to undermine your credibility. As I increased my visibility, these detractors—often referred to as trolls on the internet—emerged, attempting to publicly demean me, motivated by nothing but animosity. In these moments, the urge to withdraw and silence myself was strong. A single negative comment would make me think, *Why bother sharing anything if this is the response?* It felt as though the negative comments, despite being far fewer, would cast a shadow over the positive ones.

When we aspire to live a life echoing Christ's virtue, we should remember what He went through during His time on earth. Jesus acted in absolute obedience to God yet found Himself in a world that consistently turned its back on Him. He brought healing, hope, and redemption but was often met with rejection. So, when I strive to do good and face resistance, I'm reminded that I walk in the footsteps of the greatest figure of love and sacrifice. If the world once rejected Him, it's no wonder that those of us choosing to live by His principles might feel levels of rejection from this world too. As long as you remain grounded in love and truth, people will always have something to say. They'll be quick to envy the influence from your anointing. And when they realize that they cannot have what's designated for you, they'll try to validate their desire by arguing why you should not possess it either.

Believers in Christ are called to a standard that might often conflict with worldly values, perspectives, and priorities. But this shouldn't be a surprise because even Jesus warned His disciples that they would face difficulties and opposition because of their association with Him. Just as He was rejected and persecuted, He told them to expect similar treatment. In John 15:18-19, Jesus told them:

"If the world hates you, keep in mind that it hated me first. If you belonged to the world, it would love you as its own. As it is, you do not belong to the world, but I have chosen you out of the world. That is why the world hates you."

This warning wasn't only for His immediate disciples but for all who would choose to follow Him in the future, including modern-day believers. This serves as a heads-up to all Christians to be prepared for challenges and opposition simply because of your faith.

THE BATTLE IS NOT YOURS

As I gained a deeper understanding of God's favor, I learned to navigate a world where criticism, especially about our imperfections, is common. My growing social media presence brought more critiques about my identity, appearance, and advice. However, being aligned with God's purpose means having His support. He turns challenges into opportunities for favor. There were times when it seemed like negativity was winning, but God used those situations for my benefit. This reminds me of what Joseph told his brothers in Genesis 50:20 (NIV), "You intended to harm me, but God intended it for good to accomplish what is now being done, the saving of many lives." Through this, I experienced how adversity can be a stepping stone to greater things.

Interestingly, the videos that garnered disparaging comments were the ones that went viral, inadvertently extending my message's reach. The debates sparked by these negative remarks only served to enhance the post's visibility, turning intended reputational harm into unexpected amplification. They unknowingly helped more people see my videos. Even in moments when it seemed like the enemy had me depleted, God was strategically broadening my impact, reminding me that with faithfulness to my purpose, what's meant for harm can indeed be transformed into benefit. If I had let negative comments stop me, many people might have missed out on valuable insights. At first, I tried to address and clear up misunderstandings. But I learned from God that not all criticism needs a response. Take King Saul, for example. Even after he was anointed, many doubted and belittled him, judging him by their standards instead of recognizing God's choice. As 1 Samuel 10:27 shows, Saul responded by ignoring their insults and staying silent, showing the strength found in restraint and faith.

Just as Saul wisely chose to ignore disparaging remarks, I realized the value of doing the same. Often, when you're committed to serving, there's a natural urge to make sure your message is understood and accepted. However, God taught me two key lessons: First, Jesus never let debates about His identity or actions derail His mission. Throughout His earthly ministry, He frequently chose not to engage in confrontational arguments, exemplified by His silence during His trial before Pilate, as described in Matthew 27:14 (ESV), where "He gave him no answer, not even to a single charge, so that the governor was greatly amazed." This teaches us the power of staying focused on our purpose, not on justifying ourselves to others.

◇◇◇◇◇◇◇◇◇◇◇◇◇◇◇◇◇◇◇◇◇◇◇◇◇◇◇◇◇◇◇◇◇◇◇◇◇

Our primary aim? To remain diligent and ensure our divine purpose does what it's been created to do.

Secondly, I came to understand that I'm not accountable for others' choices. While I can offer wisdom, the responsibility for the decisions people make with it is not mine. The burden of over-explaining or trying to influence someone's path or convince them to make choices is not part of my mission. This realization was liberating. This is why it's critical to remember that our journey isn't solely about us, our feelings, or our perceptions. Our primary aim? To remain diligent and ensure our divine purpose does what it's been created to do.

A LIFE LESSON FROM DEION SANDERS

I stumbled upon a video of Deion Sanders during a press conference, and I felt as though he were speaking directly to me. Deion Sanders is a retired American athlete who played both football and baseball at the professional level. Known for his flashy personality and confident playing style, he earned the nickname "Prime Time." He is considered one of the greatest football cornerbacks in NFL history. While I missed the initial question that prompted his response during the interview, it didn't matter because what I heard was all that I needed to hear. During the live press conference, he said:

What makes you think that I care about your opinion of me? Your opinion of me is not the opinion that I have of myself. You ain't make me, so you can't break me. You didn't build me so you can't kill me. . . . God established me, so there ain't nothing you can do to me. . . . I'm not even playing the game anymore, and you've got an opinion of me. I'm not even on the field . . . [but] I love it, but I don't care. And I wish the world thought like that. Youngsters, if you're out there right now, do not give a darn what opinions people have of you as long as that opinion is not consistent with that of yourself.

You be you. I'm not playing to make you feel good about me. I already feel good about me; I'm good.[12]

All I could think to myself at that moment was, *I hear you, God.* Doesn't it say so much about God's love for us when He speaks right at the time you need to hear it most? So, what I did next I would encourage you to do too.

PERSONALIZE YOUR DECLARATIONS

Earlier, we discussed the profound power of words. And while it's easy to search the internet for ready-made affirmations or buy books filled with them, that is just scratching the surface. The real power lies in writing your own. This has become my practice: Whenever I come across a Bible verse, an inspirational quote that resonates with me, or a revelation at a pivotal moment, I transform that spark into a personal declaration. I write it down and vocalize it, turning to it whenever I need a reminder of my intrinsic worth and greatness.

So, in the case of Deion's press conference, I found that video clip, listened to it again, and transcribed it. And from that, I created my own declaration. Whenever I am feeling the weight of other people's hurtful comments beginning to creep in, I log off, go to my notes, and recite his statement that I've remixed as my personal declaration. I say:

What would lead anyone to believe that their opinion of me holds any significance? Their opinions do not validate me; I am the sole narrator of my story. Not a single individual propagating hate has played a role in the success I've achieved or the initiatives I'm birthing. They neither constructed me

12 Zairethinker, "Deion Sanders on the importance of not caring about anyone's opinion," *YouTube*, Aug. 4, 2023, Video, 1:12. https://www.youtube.com/watch?v=X_ZfZbx2V2A.

nor can they dismantle me; they didn't create me, so they cannot obliterate me. God has fashioned me as greatness, and no words can alter what He has already ordained. I am a trailblazer, a difference-maker, an indispensable asset in my field. I will not neglect my audience because of their ignorance. Opinions will surface, regardless of my actions, but I remain steadfast in my identity and unwavering in my purpose. My prayer for them is that they discover their own.

I urge you to take a moment and write down your personal declaration to address the unfounded opinions of others because let me be candid. Words have the power to wound; they hurt. This is why it's crucial for you to arm yourself with affirming words, ready to combat any negativity that tries to creep in. Crafting this declaration isn't to answer your critics but to fortify your spirit, to echo your greatness, and to audibly declare it, setting a prophetic proclamation into your atmosphere.

chapter 13

ESTABLISHMENT: YOUR GREATNESS FORTIFIES YOUR BUSINESS

*T*here's a saying often attributed to Confucius that goes, "Choose a job you love, and you will never have to work a day in your life." Now, imagine going a step further by embodying who you are and embranding your identity as your profession. At this juncture, it's no longer about just doing; it's about being. It's not work; it's a living lifestyle that naturally fuels your ambition. You're not just engaged in working a job but living out a profession that perfectly aligns with your distinguished identity.

◇◇◇◇◇◇◇◇◇◇◇◇◇◇◇◇◇◇◇◇◇◇◇◇◇◇◇◇◇◇◇◇◇◇

When your purpose becomes intertwined with your business, money doesn't need to be chased—it will find its way to you.

While it's true that businesses aim to make money, the heart of your enterprise should not be simply financial gain. When your purpose becomes intertwined with your business, money doesn't need to be chased—it will find its way to you. Aligning your identity with your brand ensures that your business isn't just a venture; it's an amplification of your reach.

MONETIZING YOUR BRAND

Recall our earlier discussion about formulating your Personal Brand Statement. This statement doesn't just represent you, but it also lays the groundwork for your entire business operation. For instance, because my Personal Brand Statement involves "inspiring greatness and success," it's only fitting that the products and services my business offers should guide individuals to recognize their own Greatness and set them on the path to success. And since this brand statement is a true reflection of who I am, running the business feels less like work and more like living.

Translating the components of your Personal Brand Statement, you could establish one or several businesses, depending on whom your products or services are tailored for. In my case, I have taken my statement of "inspiring greatness and success" and channeled it into multiple ventures. Through The HR Plug, I inspire workplaces to operate in greatness, thereby facilitating business success. Similarly, The Greatness Lab aims to encourage individuals to live out their inherent Greatness to achieve success in life. This multifaceted approach ensures a fluid, almost effortless operational flow because it is rooted in the same foundational principle of "inspiring greatness and success," which is aligned with the personal brand of who I am and what I represent.

Earlier, I pointed out a common misstep many entrepreneurs make: they rush to brand their businesses, obsessing over names, colors, and logos. However, the true initial focus should be on personal branding. A business is just a source of revenue—one of many that can be developed first by centering your efforts on becoming clear about your identity and purpose. When your business is rooted in your identity and purpose, it ensures consistency in messaging, enabling people to recognize and connect with you before they engage with what you offer. When people become connected with who you are, this familiarity translates to trust. This trust is invaluable, as people prefer to buy from those they know and trust rather than a faceless entity in an already oversaturated market. Sustainable business—it's not just about the product or service; it's about the person responsible for creating the product or service. As a result, personal branding becomes the gateway to a more authentic and sustainable business strategy.

ZUCKERBERG'S VISION: A SEAMLESS FUSION OF BRAND AND PURPOSE

Mark Zuckerberg is an acclaimed technology entrepreneur and co-founder of Facebook, Inc. Today, Zuckerberg wears multiple hats as the chairman, CEO, and controlling shareholder of what has evolved into Meta Platforms, Inc. In a strategic move to rival another social media company called Twitter, Zuckerberg unveiled a new platform in July 2023 under the Meta brand called "Threads." This innovative space prioritizes text-based conversations to facilitate real-time interactions. The reception was astronomical: within a mere forty-eight hours, Threads saw over seventy million people register to use the platform. Such a staggering response was not predominantly driven by fully understanding Threads' functionalities but was influenced by the reputation, credibility, and trust of the innovative genius Zuckerberg has proved himself to be because of his success with Facebook.

Mark Zuckerberg's journey reveals a profound insight: his vision for Facebook, realized shortly after its launch in 2004, was always about more than a social network. It was about connecting communities globally. This larger mission to catalyze global change through community connections was clearly articulated in his 2017 Harvard commencement speech. He emphasized that change begins locally yet has the potential to grow globally, starting "with people like us." Reflecting on Facebook's origins, he described how it began with connecting communities in a dorm room, laying the groundwork for his ambition to connect the entire world.

Mark Zuckerberg's personal brand and his business endeavors, including Facebook, Messenger, WhatsApp, and Instagram, all share a common thread: his commitment to global community connections. Each platform, whether it's WhatsApp with its multimedia messaging capabilities or Instagram with its focus on photo and video sharing, aligns with his vision of bringing people together. In Zuckerberg's approach to business, it's clear that his decisions are not solely about market opportunities but are deeply rooted in his purpose. Every new venture or acquisition is more than a business move; it's an extension of his personal mission to connect communities worldwide.

Zuckerberg's path to success is rooted in principles that resonate with his business and personal brand. Understanding his background and the trajectory of his success makes his journey relatable and inspiring to others with similar aspirations. Knowing that he achieved monumental success without a traditional college degree or formal training can be incredibly motivating. It shows that unconventional paths can lead to extraordinary outcomes. This is precisely why the "how" of your journey is crucial. It underscores the importance of aligning your business endeavors with your personal purpose. Your story, much like Zuckerberg's, is not just about what you achieve but about how you navigate your path, overcome obstacles, and stay true to your purpose. This alignment makes your business more than a venture; it becomes a reflection of your identity and mission. It becomes the "Business of You."

True alignment of personal brand with purpose in business, as demonstrated by Zuckerberg, means maintaining a consistent essence across all ventures. Rather than starting from scratch with each new project, the core of the brand persists, making every new undertaking a logical extension of the last. For Zuckerberg, this means continually focusing on uniting people within a global community. His steadfast dedication to this mission is a defining feature of his career. The motto of Meta—"Giving people the power to build community and bring the world closer together"—is more than just a slogan. It's a clear reflection of Zuckerberg's unwavering commitment to his foundational purpose.

OPRAH'S LEGACY: BRANDING THE ESSENCE OF YOU

Let's contemplate another compelling instance of impeccable branding: Oprah Winfrey. Oprah isn't merely a name; it's a brand, a movement, a verb in the dictionary of popular culture. The moment we hear her name, we don't just think of her TV show or any single endeavor. Instead, we think of Oprah, the person—her values, her philanthropy, her journey, and her authenticity. The mere utterance of "Oprah" shows varying emotions, memories, and associations for people worldwide. She has successfully created a brand that is directly aligned with who she is as a person.

Oprah's audiences don't just love her; they trust her. People buy into her offerings not merely as consumers but as followers of a person whose authenticity they trust and respect. Her personal brand sells whatever products she launches as a business. People buy a product or tune into a show because it has Oprah's name attached; they do so because they trust her judgment, resonate with her values, and believe in what she represents. That's the potency of personal branding. But how did she manage to transform her name into such an influential brand?

Starting from her roots in a humble Mississippi town, Oprah's life story has been one of resilience, grit, and transformation. Her early years in television paved the way, but it was her authentic approach to communication, her vulnerability in sharing her own struggles, and her genuine empathy that endeared her to millions. *The Oprah Winfrey Show* didn't just dominate the daytime talk show realm for a quarter-century; it revolutionized it. Here was a platform where real issues met real emotions, where guests and audiences felt seen and heard.

As the years went by, her personal brand only grew stronger. Oprah's personal brand isn't just about commercialism but is more so an extension of her authentic self, which naturally translates into her various business ventures. Oprah wasn't just a TV host; she was a symbol of hope, inspiration, and positive change. This powerful personal brand laid the foundation for a multitude of successful ventures. From the influential *O, The Oprah Magazine,* to the OWN Network, from her role as a producer and actress in various movies to her philanthropic endeavors, every venture seemed to bear the essence of who Oprah was and what she stood for.

◇◇◇◇◇◇◇◇◇◇◇◇◇◇◇◇◇◇◇◇◇◇◇◇◇◇◇◇◇◇◇◇

When you embed your authentic self into what you do, your personal brand becomes powerful enough to dominate individual ventures

And while there might be a multitude of businesses and initiatives under her umbrella that people aren't necessarily aware of, the name "Oprah" is universally recognized. This is the power of a strong brand: her name alone has become the entity. Every venture, whether directly or indirectly, draws from the wellspring of authenticity, passion, and commitment that is Oprah. Oprah's journey teaches us that when you embed your authentic self into what you do, your personal brand becomes powerful enough to dominate individual ventures. It's not about the individual products or shows; it's about the emotional connection. That is the genius of Oprah's brand, and why she remains an example of how moving in her designed Greatness has sustained her.

WHAT IS THE BUSINESS OF YOU?

When it comes to business, I encourage you to challenge the conventional sense that it's solely about offering a product or service to meet a need. Instead, I want you to think of business as the strategic art of packaging and showcasing your identity to the world. It's the formal stamp on a program, process, or product tailored especially for a specific audience. They need to comprehend your journey and the challenges you've overcome, so they, too, can find the strength to persist. This perspective allows others to truly value and benefit from you and your story. Business then becomes more than just about a product or service; it's becoming the authentic *you* ingrained in that offering: the Business of You. Just as when Oprah endorses something it carries weight and trust, your unique imprint will evoke similar trust and resonance. When people understand and connect with your story, they are more likely to trust and seek what you uniquely bring to the table.

◇◇◇◇◇◇◇◇◇◇◇◇◇◇◇◇◇◇◇◇◇◇◇◇◇◇◇◇◇◇◇◇

I want you to think of business as the strategic art of packaging and showcasing your identity to the world.

Ensuring that who you profess to be aligns seamlessly with what you offer is the art and science of branding. Take a moment to consider this: when you see a checkmark logo accompanied by the phrase Just Do It," which brand springs to mind? Most people would instantly think of Nike. Now, if you delve deeper and ask what Nike's brand is, the immediate response might lean toward sneakers since that's what they're renowned for selling. However, Nike offers so much more than just athletic footwear. At its core, Nike sells hope and embodies the mantra "Just Do It"—it's a motivational brand that permeates every product and campaign. When you think of "Just Do It," it's more than a slogan; it's a call to stop hesitating, to stop doubting, and to commence acting—that is the brand of Nike.

Nike's brand story originates from its founder's frustration with excuses and obstacles. He built and defined businesses that mirrored his identity and values—values of endurance, motivation, and inspiration to "Just Do It." Now, any product or campaign tied to perseverance, especially from a fitness or sports perspective, evokes the name Nike. Competitors like Adidas and Puma might also sell athletic gear, but when it comes to the concept of pushing boundaries and persevering, that's the connection point for Nike. That is the power of precise and purposeful branding aligned with your identity.

As a founder, everything connected to who you are—your missions and your values—becomes integral to your offerings. When people trust your brand, they don't second-guess the quality or relevance of your offerings. Consumers of Nike won't question if those sneakers will properly support their feet or if that attire is suitable for their golf game. Why? Because their trust isn't just in the product but in—the brand. I won't interrogate any aspect of what you offer as a business or service once your brand has garnered my trust.

It's crucial to realize that our own self-worth, our personal brand, often holds more weight than the businesses we create. That's where sustainability comes from—not the products but the person. And that's why an emphasis should be on crafting and marketing our identities, ensuring people understand and resonate with who we are. Once that connection is established, they'll naturally be inclined to invest in what you do.

◇◇◇◇◇◇◇◇◇◇◇◇◇◇◇◇◇◇◇◇◇◇◇◇◇◇◇◇◇◇◇◇◇

Our own self-worth, our personal brand, often holds more weight than the businesses we create. That's where sustainability comes from—not the products but the person.

ESTABLISHING YOUR BUSINESS

When people think about the concept of business, the first thing they are often told is that their business needs to be established. But what does that really mean, and why is it such an important step? In the world of business, establishment stands as a sign of legitimacy, trust, and stability. A well-established business provides a clear direction rooted in its mission, vision, and values, ensures dependable operational structures, and lays the groundwork for lasting success. So, to achieve success in business, establishment is key. Likewise, if "you" are the business, you, too, must be firmly established to succeed. However, the establishment for an individual isn't just about brand visibility or market dominance. It's much deeper than that.

When we talk about you as the business, being established means diving deep into your identity, understanding your purpose, and aligning with it. In Hosea 2:23 (GNT), where the Lord says, "I will establish my people in the land and make them prosper," the emphasis is on "my people"—those who first acknowledge they belong to Him. God specifically establishes those who embrace and accept the divine assignment of their identity and purpose in Him. This alignment, according to scripture, is key to being truly established. It suggests that as you unfold and embrace your God-given identity, you authentically engage with your divine purpose. This isn't just about fulfilling worldly roles; it's about living in harmony with God's will. Such alignment leads to a profound establishment, one that brings not only worldly success but also deep, sustainable prosperity grounded in divine purpose.

So, in carving out your business path through the lens of your God-given identity, understanding that you're already established by Him becomes pivotal. Establishment transitions from being more than just a business principle to becoming a spiritual journey where your identity, purpose, and business become a testament to living in the path that God has laid out for you. In this confluence of divinity and entrepreneurship, business isn't just a commercial entity but a fulfilled destiny where every product, service, and connection becomes a manifestation of your purpose. As you embrace your divine establishment, you'll find that not only do doors open and opportunities manifest, but there's a sense of fulfillment and contentment that is greater than mere business success.

In shaping your business according to your God-given identity, recognizing your divine establishment becomes crucial. This transforms the concept of establishment from a mere business principle to a spiritual journey. In this journey, your identity, purpose, and business activities become a living testament to fulfilling the design of your God-given DNA. Within this fusion of faith and entrepreneurship, your business transcends being just a commercial venture; it becomes the embodiment of your destiny. Every product, service, and interaction reflects your purpose and God's plan. As you embrace this divine establishment, you'll discover that it not only opens doors and creates opportunities but also brings a sense of fulfillment and contentment far surpassing conventional business success.

YOUR GREATNESS ESTABLISHES YOU

The word "establish" holds great significance in the Bible, often conveying the idea of bringing about stability, permanence, and a firm foundation. It is used to describe how God establishes His covenant with His people, how He establishes His kingdom, and how believers are called to establish their faith. In Proverbs 16:3 (NIV), God assures us that when we fully commit our plans to Him, He will establish them.

God promises to establish our plans, to put the right plans for us in our hearts when we go all in—commit to him every day. By the way, commitment doesn't mean perfection; rather, it's about consistently offering our utmost, striving diligently to embrace righteousness while distancing ourselves from things and people who are enemies to our success.

◇◇◇◇◇◇◇◇◇◇◇◇◇◇◇◇◇◇◇◇◇◇◇◇◇◇◇◇◇

Commitment doesn't mean perfection; rather, it's about consistently offering our utmost, striving diligently to embrace righteousness while distancing ourselves from things and people who are enemies to your success.

Embracing your role as an established follower of Christ means releasing worries about business outcomes. When your business strategy aligns with God's plan, its success is not just a possibility but an inevitability. Prosperity and success are outcomes of this divine alignment. This journey is more than business; it's a deep exploration of your true identity which in turn illuminates your life's path. Jeremiah 29:11 (NIV) echoes this sentiment: "For I know the plans I have for you," declares the Lord, "plans to prosper you and not to harm you, plans to give you hope and a future." Aligning with God's plan ensures success. Whenever worry arises, replace it with worship and trust in His promise of prosperity.

In your journey, always remember that when you're passionately pursuing your purpose, the right people will find their way to you. The book of Luke provides a beautiful testament to this. As Jesus stepped into the fullness of His purpose, healing the sick and preaching the Good News, the scriptures tell us: "But the news about Him was spreading farther, and large crowds kept gathering to hear Him and to be healed of their illnesses" (Luke 5:15, AMP). The use of the word "kept" when describing those gathering to hear him underscores a vital point—it wasn't a singular event but a continuous attraction. People were not just once—but continually—drawn toward Him simply because He was fulfilling His assignment. This illustrates that when you're executing work that is assigned to you, work that transforms lives, you will attract the people, clients, customers—those called to you. There's no need for elaborate marketing campaigns or persistent advertising. All you need to do is stay true to who God has called you to be, and the rest will follow. Your purposeful work becomes your most genuine and powerful attractor.

◇◇◇◇◇◇◇◇◇◇◇◇◇◇◇◇◇◇◇◇◇◇◇◇◇◇◇◇◇◇

Whenever worry arises, replace it with worship and trust in His promise of prosperity.

NAVIGATING THE BUSINESS OF YOU: EMBRACING THE PILLARS OF SUSTAINABLE IMPACT

A business rooted in your distinguished greatness—the unshakeable foundation of your identity—is destined for unfailing success. Remember, Greatness is your DNA because you come from the

Greatest, and within you lies an indomitable spirit and unimaginable potential. Outlined below are five pivotal pillars, constituting a framework to ensure your business strategy proves purposeful for your assignment. By connecting your business to these foundational pillars, the Business of You becomes not just a venture but a voyage where your identity doesn't merely shape your business but ensures profitability and everlasting impact. Each of these pillars holds distinct significance, yet together, they form a cohesive foundation that strengthens and supports the overall structure of your business.

PILLAR #1: ALIGNMENT

The foremost pillar in your spiritual business plan is ensuring alignment with God's vision in every business decision. It's a partnership where He provides the plan for your journey, and you act as the executor, bringing this vision into reality. Prayer stands as the essential communication channel with God. It is through prayer that you seek guidance for your business decisions, striving to align them with His divine plan. This process involves not only speaking to God but also listening attentively for His response.

By incorporating prayer into your decision-making process, you open yourself to receiving His wisdom and direction. This also helps in protecting your business from potential missteps and failures. Before taking any action, ensure that you have sought His counsel through prayer and have received a sense of confirmation or direction. Prayerful discernment ensures that each step you take in your business is in harmony with God's vision, thus maintaining a strong alignment with His purpose for you.

PILLAR #2: AUTHENTICITY

Brands grounded in authenticity forge deeper, more meaningful connections, cultivating trust and loyalty among customers. By embracing and sharing your unique story and perspective, your business distinguishes itself in a crowded marketplace, naturally reducing competition. Authenticity means genuinely representing yourself, ensuring that what your business offers is a true reflection of your identity and consistently aligns with the values you uphold. To uphold this authenticity, engage in regular self-reflection to ensure your business practices and communications genuinely mirror your identity and values. It's about being honest with yourself about what you stand for and how these principles are reflected in your business practices and offerings. Transparency with your audience, sharing both triumphs and challenges, further solidifies this authenticity. This means being open about your journey, including the successes and the challenges, and consistently presenting your true self to your customers. By intertwining self-reflection and openness in your routine, your brand maintains its authentic character, resonating with and earning the trust of your audience.

PILLAR #3: APPROACH

Your business approach should be grounded in a mindset that aligns with Philippians 2:3-4 (NIV), which urges us:

> Do nothing out of selfish ambition or vain conceit. Rather, in humility value others above yourselves, not looking to your own interests but each of you to the interests of the others.

This scripture underlines the importance of prioritizing the needs and well-being of your audience in every interaction. Consistency in how you engage with clients and customers, guided by a spirit of service and love, is essential. Such an approach, mindful of serving others before self, not only reflects your brand's authenticity but also ensures that your business operations are aligned with your purpose, which is ultimately for the benefit of those you serve. Adopting an approach of humility and service, as commanded in the teachings of Christ, sets you apart in a world often characterized by self-centeredness.

It's not just about having a plan that aligns with God's assignment for you but also ensuring your approach in business reflects the way He instructs us to serve others. This alignment in both plan and practice not only makes your business stand out but also ensures it operates on principles that are counter to the norm yet deeply impactful. By doing so, you create an environment where your business isn't just a commercial entity but represents the values and principles taught by Christ, drawing others to want to come know Him because of their experience with you.

PILLAR #4: ADAPTABILITY

The key to adaptability in business lies in a combination of strategies that ensure your business grows and evolves with your personal journey. By integrating these suggestive approaches, you create a business environment that is not only adaptable but also primed for continuous growth and evolution. First, know that continuous learning is essential. Staying updated with the latest trends, skills, and knowledge in your industry through reading, attending seminars, and engaging with new research keeps your strategies fresh and relevant. Secondly, soliciting regular feedback and conducting evaluations of your business processes is vital. This feedback loop can reveal areas for improvement and innovation, helping you stay agile and responsive. Networking is another crucial element. Building relationships with other professionals and entrepreneurs can provide new perspectives, ideas, and opportunities that foster adaptability. Utilizing technology effectively is another key aspect. Embracing technological advancements can streamline operations, expand your reach, and give you a competitive edge. A mindset open to change is also critical for adaptability. Being mindful and receptive to changing circumstances and willing to implement necessary changes keeps your business agile. Consulting with mentors, business coaches, or industry experts can also guide your decisions and strategies, ensuring that your business remains adaptable and aligned with your evolving personal journey.

PILLAR #5: APTITUDE

Aptitude in business involves resilience, adaptability, and a strong emotional and spiritual intelligence needed in navigating the business world. It's about developing the inner strength and mindset to see challenges as growth opportunities, ensuring your business is not just resilient but also evolving. Key practices for building aptitude include developing emotional intelligence to enhance empathy and decision-making, cultivating resilience to positively navigate business ups and downs, and prioritizing self-care for a balanced and healthy approach to work. By focusing on these aspects, you strengthen your ability to respond to challenges effectively, align your actions with your spiritual values, and maintain a steady focus on your purpose.

To ensure aptitude in your business, focus on a few key practices such as developing your emotional intelligence. This means becoming more aware and understanding of both your own emotions and those of others around you. Prioritizing self-care and wellness is also essential. Maintaining a balance between work and personal life, ensuring physical health through exercise and proper diet, and mental well-being through stress management and relaxation techniques are all vital. A sound mind and body are critical for making clear, effective decisions and sustaining the energy and focus required for long-term business success. By focusing on these aspects, you strengthen your ability to respond to challenges effectively, align your actions with your spiritual values, and maintain a steady focus on your purpose.

Focusing on the business of you prioritizes God's plan for you. You've already been established; the hard part is down. Now, it's about living your life to tell your story for the betterment of others. This holistic approach to business is about more than just financial success; it's about building a legacy that reflects your deepest values and positively impacts the world around you. When this strategy becomes the core foundation of your enterprise, you will experience profitability with lasting impact and relevance.

chapter 14

RELATIONSHIPS: YOUR GREATNESS FORGES VALUABLE CONNECTIONS

*E*mbracing your distinguished identity often means parting ways with aspects of your old life—certain people, relationships, familiar spaces, and even material things. This transformation may distance you from comfort zones and familiarity. It's a path where some relationships might dissolve, and friends who don't understand the "new you" might drift away or even speak negatively about you. You might find yourself misunderstood by relatives and judged by people who once thought highly of you.

However, I urge you not to let these changes discourage you. Change is a natural part of life's journey. The Bible, in Ecclesiastes 3:1 (AMP), reminds us, "There is a season (a time appointed) for everything and a time for every delight *and* event *or* purpose under heaven." This verse speaks to the ebb and flow of life, where each relationship, experience, and phase has its appointed time. Just as seasons change in nature, so do seasons in our lives. Some relationships might be for a specific period, serving a purpose for that particular phase of growth. The relationship ending doesn't signify failure or loss; rather, it's a transition into a new season, bringing different opportunities and relationships that align more closely with your current path. Embracing this concept helps in accepting the natural progression of relationships without disappointment. Because as you evolve, so do your relationship needs. Trusting in this process is trusting in God's divine timing and plan for your life.

◇◇◇◇◇◇◇◇◇◇◇◇◇◇◇◇◇◇◇◇◇◇◇◇◇◇◇◇◇◇◇◇◇◇◇◇

At the Pinnacle of Greatness, you'll attract new people into your life—those who genuinely understand and appreciate you for who you are and what you bring to the world.

At the Pinnacle of Greatness, you'll attract new people into your life—those who genuinely understand and appreciate you for who you are and what you bring to the world. The connections you forge will be based on authenticity and mutual respect. You'll no longer concern yourself with those who don't resonate with who you are because you'll be surrounded by individuals who appreciate your presence. You'll soon find comfort becomes secondary to purpose. You'll find yourself continuously driven, seeking to serve more people. You'll recognize operating in Greatness is where true success lies—in the impact and assistance you provide to others. Remember, everything you leave behind belongs to the person you once were. Now, it's time to fully embrace the person you were designed to be. This journey is not just about personal achievement; it's about learning the strategy to contribute meaningfully and live life on your terms.

Along with changes in your external relationships, be prepared to face internal emotional and psychological challenges that may arise on your journey of self-discovery. As you embrace the new you, you may find that what was once familiar, or what you believed was your destiny, no longer feels fulfilling. Skills you've honed and mastered over the years might suddenly seem less satisfying. This change in perception is a natural part of your transformation. You'll begin to realize that purpose and success aren't solely about financial gain or personal accolades; they're about fulfilling the needs of those who require your unique talents and value contributions. It's a shift from a self-centered view of success to one that's centered on serving God and others. You may find yourself walking away from well-paying jobs, not because they aren't valuable but because they don't align with the deeper calling you've discovered. This transition is about aligning your professional life with the purpose you were created for, even if it means leaving behind what was once comfortable and familiar.

TODD DULANEY'S STORY: LIVING IN TRUE PURPOSE

Growing up, Todd Dulaney envisioned a career in professional baseball, a dream that began to materialize when he was drafted by the New York Mets in 2002. Despite his talent and potential in baseball, a profound experience at a church service led him to reassess his life's direction. Dulaney realized that his heart was being pulled toward a different calling—a life dedicated to faith and gospel music. Dulaney's journey wasn't just about changing careers; it was about aligning his life with what he believed he was purposed for. After leaving baseball in 2005, he transitioned into music, eventually becoming a Grammy-nominated gospel artist himself. Dulaney's story is a testament to the importance of listening to your inner calling and having the courage to follow it, even when it means leaving behind a familiar and established path. His journey highlights that true fulfillment comes not from external success but from aligning your life with your purpose in God's plan.

As we reflect on Dulaney's journey, I'd like for you to take a moment and consider your own path. Are you pursuing a career or a lifestyle because it's what you truly feel called to do? Or are you settled in what's familiar, guided by the allure of comfort and societal expectations? Ask yourself: *Am I willing to make bold moves to align my career and life with purpose?* Remember, it's never too late to realign your journey with your authentic calling, and in doing so, you open yourself up to a life of deeper satisfaction and purpose.

Dulaney's inspiring journey from professional baseball to gospel music provides a compelling example of what following purpose over more conventional paths of success looks like. But the decision to transition from baseball to gospel music was not easy. Dulaney faced skepticism and disbelief, especially from those who saw baseball as a more lucrative and prestigious path. He said:

> *My family and friends thought I was crazy for leaving baseball. But I knew that is what I needed to do and what I wanted to do. I wanted to give myself to the wholehearted pursuit of God, so that is what I did—and I never looked back.* [13]

---

13 Kymberlee Norswo, "Gospel Artist Todd Dulaney Traded His Professional Baseball Career for a Life of Faith," *Andscape*, 2 Dec. 2018, andscape.com/features/gospel-artist-todd-dulaney-traded-his-professional-baseball-career-for-a-life-of-faith/.

YOUR RELATIONSHIP CIRCLE: PROXIMITY, ACCESS, AND INFLUENCE

The "Relationship Circle" is a dynamic map of the individuals in your life, arrayed according to their proximity to the center where you stand. This arrangement reflects the level of access and time each person receives from you. Those closer to the center have a greater influence and a more direct role in your life, garnering more of your time and attention. They are typically the ones you turn to for frequent support, guidance, and interaction. Conversely, those positioned further from the center have less access and receive less time, reflecting their lesser role or influence in your daily affairs. Managing this Circle effectively means being mindful of who you allow in these inner and outer rings, ensuring that those closest to you are those who truly align with and support your personal and professional growth.

◇◇◇◇◇◇◇◇◇◇◇◇◇◇◇◇◇◇◇◇◇◇◇◇◇◇◇◇◇◇◇◇◇◇

This arrangement of people in your Relationship Circle reflects the level of access and time each person receives from you. Those closer to the center have a greater influence and a more direct role in your life, garnering more of your time and attention.

If you find yourself uncertain or struggling to decide your next steps, consider the significance of the people in your Circle—those who have access to you and into whom you invest your time and energy. Consider Todd Dulaney's journey—the time and emotional energy he might have invested in explaining his career shift and the friends he may have lost along the way. Surrounding yourself with the right people is crucial as these relationships significantly impact your personal and professional growth. The right individuals can offer support and understanding for transformative decisions, as Dulaney experienced, or conversely, they can fuel doubts and hesitations, potentially causing you to miss critical opportunities for change.

YOUR RELATIONSHIP CIRCLE STARTS WITH A MENTOR

In your journey, understanding who to turn to at various stages is crucial. Overall, in constructing your Relationship Circle, various roles are essential: mentors, consultants, family, friends, sponsors, coaches, and risk management professionals like lawyers and accountants. Be mindful of who these people are because placing your energy into people who focus on why you can't succeed—rather than believing in your potential—will drain you. It's important to identify and distance yourself from these "enemies" of your progress. Actively choose to delete, unfriend, unfollow, block, erase, and disconnect from anyone who diminishes your peace, love, and happiness and imposes doubt to weaken your faith.

As you assess the people in your life, identifying who stays, who joins, and who leaves, prioritize finding a mentor. A mentor is more than an advisor; they're a personal ally who truly believes in you and your purpose. Their guidance and insights can be invaluable, not only in your personal and professional growth but also in helping you discern which individuals in your Circle might be hindering your progress and need to be let go. They are a source of wisdom, support, and encouragement, helping you to see beyond immediate challenges and focus on long-term goals. Mentorship is about having someone who inspires you to realize your own potential and supports you in reaching it. They often see more in you than you see in yourself and can help you unlock doors you didn't even know existed. A mentor's belief in your abilities and commitment to your growth can be a powerful driver for easing discomforts that are common with the changes you will experience in this journey.

The other roles you should identify in your Circle serve distinct but equally vital purposes: Strategists help you devise and implement plans to achieve specific goals. Sponsors use their influence to advance your career. Coaches focus on developing your skills and capabilities. And professionals like lawyers and accountants help manage risks and ensure the stability and legality of your endeavors. Each of these roles contributes uniquely to your journey, but it is the mentor who often plays the most transformative role in your personal and professional evolution. Their guidance is not just about imparting knowledge; it's about fostering your growth, belief in yourself, and alignment with your purpose.

THE MISCONCEPTION ABOUT A COACH

Consider the role of a coach in a sports team. They are there to motivate, encourage, and inspire the players. Coaches push athletes to their limits during practice and help them adhere to a disciplined regimen essential for their chosen sport. However, a coach's role is not to decide whether a sport is right for a player. They work to bring out the best in a player based on the player's aspirations and commitment. If a player isn't meeting performance standards, it might lead to them being benched or cut from the team, but these consequences stem from performance, not from a deeper assessment of the player's personal alignment with the sport.

Many often seek a coach when they feel guidance is needed, but the role of a consultant or strategist should not be overlooked. A coach is excellent for enhancing skills and achieving specific goals, providing support and accountability. However, their focus is not typically on redirecting you to a path that aligns with your deeper purpose or calling. Many perceive me as a coach, but my role is quite different. While coaches are crucial for goal achievement, I operate as a strategist. This role goes beyond just supporting a person's aspirations; it's about guiding them toward where they're truly meant to be. As a strategist, I offer direct advice and specific recommendations, aligning your journey with your authentic purpose and destiny. Rather than just supporting your chosen direction, I help you discover and follow your ultimate path, providing necessary correction and strategic insight.

Through the process we've outlined so far, you'll realize that before seeking a coach, a strategist and a mentor can be more beneficial. Coaches are most effective once you have a clear understanding of where you're supposed to go. A strategist and mentor will guide you to discover and align with your path, and then once discovered, a coach helps you thrive within that path. The key is to leverage the right type of relationship at the right time.

BEYOND THE YES: BE OKAY WITH BEING CHALLENGED

In the journey of personal and professional growth, it's vital to avoid the trap of surrounding yourself with "yes" people. True leaders and inquisitive learners recognize the value of being challenged. Steve Jobs, the co-founder of Apple, famously valued employees who could challenge his thinking. He believed that the best results come from vigorous debate and not from passive agreement. This sentiment is confirmed in the saying, "If you're the smartest person in the room, you're in the wrong room."

Operating as Greatness involves having people around you who aren't afraid to question assumptions and propose alternative solutions. This not only leads to better decision-making but also drives innovation. So, avoid surrounding yourself with people who constantly agree with you— it hinders your growth. Instead, having people who ask tough questions and offer differing viewpoints will push you out of your comfort zone, helping you explore new ideas and expand your knowledge.

CASE STUDY: DANYELLE'S BAKERY

Here's a scenario illustrating how a mentor, consultant, coach, and sponsor might each play a role in Danyelle's journey to open a bakery:

Mentor: Dany, an aspiring bakery owner, connects with Kimberly, a successful bakery owner who has been in the business for years. Kimberly provides Dany with insights into the bakery industry, shares her experiences about starting and running a bakery, and advises Dany on managing the challenges of being a new business owner. She becomes a sounding board for Dany's ideas and a source of encouragement and wisdom.

Consultant: Dany hires Ted, a restaurant launching strategist, to help develop a detailed plan for her bakery based on his experience. Ted assists in market analysis, financial planning, and setting up business operations. They work together on specific strategies for marketing, menu development, and customer engagement, ensuring that Dany's bakery has a solid plan for success.

Coach: To hone her leadership and management skills, Dany engages with Lamont, a professional coach. Lamont helps Dany set clear personal and professional goals, improve her communication skills, and develop effective team management strategies. Through regular sessions, Dany gains the confidence and skills necessary to lead her team and grow her business.

Sponsor: Dany participates in a local business association where she meets Sandy, a well-connected business leader in the community. Sandy, impressed by Dany's passion and business plan, advocates for her in the local business community. She introduces Dany to key suppliers, recommends her bakery to potential large clients for catering, and connects her with opportunities to showcase her bakery at prominent local events.

As you can see, each role contributes uniquely to Dany's journey. Her mentor provides personal insights and guidance, the consultant helps create a concrete business plan guiding her in the direction she should go, her coach aids in skill development, and her sponsor opens doors to opportunities and networks that Dany might not have accessed on her own. Together, they play a pivotal role in the successful launch and growth of Dany's bakery. Just as Dany carefully built her support system to succeed in her bakery endeavor, assessing your Relationship Circle can ensure that the people in your life align optimally with your journey toward success.

BUILDING YOUR RELATIONSHIP CIRCLE

Warren Buffett, one of the world's most successful investors, wisely observed that we are, in many ways, a reflection of the people we spend the most time with. This principle highlights the importance of choosing your Circle wisely. The people around you can either elevate your thinking, challenge you to grow, and support your progress, or they can limit your potential. By carefully selecting these individuals, you ensure that your environment is conducive to learning, growth, and success.

Beyond just choosing the right people to be in your Circle, you should be prepared to assign specific roles or "assignments" to everyone in relation to your purpose. By giving each person an assignment, you cultivate a Circle that is not just supportive but also functional and purpose-driven. For instance, one person might be your sounding board for new ideas, another could provide honest feedback, and someone else might be a source of emotional support or spiritual guidance. This strategic approach to relationships emphasizes the importance of intentionality and purpose in personal connections, suggesting a proactive method of ensuring that each relationship actively supports and contributes to your vision. When assigning roles within your Relationship Circle, consider the time and energy you invest in each person. Reflect on the nature of your interactions: Are you spending excessive time explaining or justifying your God-guided decisions? Or, perhaps, too much time convincing them of the importance of their role in your purpose?

Prioritize your time effectively. Your personal development, inherently aligned with God, should be your primary focus. Those who oppose or fail to understand your calling—the enemies of your purpose and strangers—should occupy the least amount of your time and energy. This approach ensures that your most valuable resource, time, is spent with those who genuinely support and contribute to your journey. By doing so, you maintain alignment with your purpose, avoiding the drain of unnecessary justifications or persuasions. It's a strategic way of ensuring that each relationship in your life not only serves but also enhances your pursuit of destiny.

◇◇◇◇◇◇◇◇◇◇◇◇◇◇◇◇◇◇◇◇◇◇◇◇◇◇◇◇◇◇◇◇◇◇◇

Prioritize your time effectively. Your personal development, inherently aligned with God, should be your primary focus. Those who oppose or fail to understand your calling should occupy the least amount of your time and energy.

WHO'S IN YOUR RELATIONSHIP CIRCLE?

Begin your introspective journey by evaluating the current relationships in your life. Reflect on who these individuals are and the roles they play. Are they mentors offering guidance, strategists helping chart your course, family and friends who are supportive, coaches developing your skills, sponsors advocating for you, or professionals managing your risks? Understanding each person's role is crucial in determining their alignment with your overarching vision. Here are some relationship roles to consider identifying for your Circle.

◇ Spouse
◇ Mentor
◇ Lawyer
◇ Accountant
◇ Consultant
◇ Coach
◇ Sponsor
◇ Immediate/Extended Family
◇ Friends

◇ Peers/Colleagues
◇ Enemies (of your time working toward purpose)

It's important to recognize the value and contribution of everyone in your life. Are they positively impacting your journey, challenging you constructively, and offering valuable advice, or are they draining your energy without significant return? Reflect on any gaps in your Relationship Circle. Are there roles that are currently unfulfilled but necessary for your growth and success? Perhaps you lack a mentor to guide you, a sponsor to open doors, or a coach to refine specific skills. Identifying these gaps is the first step toward filling them.

Finally, consider if some relationships need to be reassigned or let go. Not everyone currently in your life may fit in your Relationship Circle, and some may no longer serve a positive purpose on your path. This reflection is not about assigning blame but about strategically aligning your Circle with your personal and professional aspirations, ensuring that each relationship supports and enhances your journey toward success.

NO VACANCY, MY CIRCLE IS FULL

Having recognized the significance of surrounding yourself with the right circle of relationships, you might realize that some of the current relationships in your life no longer serve your growth or align with your path. This can be a challenging but necessary aspect of personal and professional development.

It's vital to recognize that some people in our lives are meant to be temporary influences rather than permanent fixtures. Those who continuously anchor you to your old self—instead of embracing the new you—ultimately do not contribute positively to your journey. They might become inadvertent adversaries, fixated on your past rather than supportive of your evolution. Failing to recognize and address this can hinder your progress, leading to stagnation or regression. It's important to have the discernment to sever ties with such individuals, ensuring that your Circle is composed of those who genuinely support and align with your current and future aspirations.

As you live and grow, certain individuals may not comprehend or appreciate the level of your growth and greatness. However, ending these dead-end relationships requires a thoughtful and respectful approach. Here are some steps to consider:

◇ Self-Reflection: Begin by reflecting on why the relationship no longer fits with your goals and values. Understanding your reasons clearly will help you communicate more effectively and stand firm in your decision.

◇ Open and Honest Communication: Have an honest conversation with the person. Express your feelings and reasons for deciding to move on in a respectful and clear manner. It's important to focus on your experiences and feelings rather than placing blame.

◇ Set Boundaries: If a complete end to the relationship isn't necessary, consider setting new boundaries that align better with your current objectives and well-being.

◇ Seek Support: Ending relationships can be emotionally taxing. Lean on your support network of trusted friends, family, or professionals for guidance and emotional support.

◇ Gradual Distancing: In some cases, a gradual distancing might be more appropriate than a direct confrontation, especially if the relationship is not deeply personal or if direct communication may lead to unnecessary conflict.

◇ Be Love: Regardless of the reasons for ending the relationship, approach the situation with empathy and kindness. Remember that this decision is about your growth and alignment, not a judgment of the other person's character or worth.

While letting go of certain relationships can be difficult, it's often a necessary step in your journey toward personal and professional fulfillment. By carefully and compassionately managing this process, you make room for new, more strategically aligned relationships that support your growth and goals.

DISCERNING THE TRUE INTENTIONS IN RELATIONSHIPS

The Bible offers clear guidance on the influence of relationships, cautioning against the dangers of associating with the wrong people. In 1 Corinthians 15:33 (AMP), we are warned, "Do not be deceived: 'Bad company corrupts good morals.'" James 4:4b (AMP) further intensifies this caution by stating, 'Whoever wishes to be a friend of the world makes himself an enemy of God." This verse underscores the spiritual risks of forming close bonds with those whose values conflict with ours. These scriptures collectively emphasize the importance of choosing relationships that uplift and align with our morals rather than those that lead us away from our spiritual path. They remind us that our associations can have profound impacts, not just on our earthly conduct but on our spiritual alignment and relationship with God.

◇◇◇◇◇◇◇◇◇◇◇◇◇◇◇◇◇◇◇◇◇◇◇◇◇◇◇◇◇◇◇

Trusting in God's love and wisdom will ultimately reveal the true nature of people's intentions.

It's crucial to turn to God for insight into the roles people play in your life. Our emotions and human nature can sometimes cloud our judgment, making it hard to see or accept the true intentions of those around us. However, trusting in God's love and wisdom will ultimately reveal the true nature of people's intentions. Here's a prayer for God's guidance in discerning and managing relationships. It's okay to be strategic, asking for the wisdom to recognize valuable connections and grace in letting go of those whose time has passed.

Heavenly Father,

I come before You, seeking wisdom and discernment in my relationships. Please guide me in surrounding myself with the right people, those who uplift, support, and align with Your purpose for my life. Grant me the insight to recognize and cherish these individuals and the strength to nurture these relationships that You have blessed me with.

Lord, I also pray for the grace to let go of relationships that have served their purpose. Help me to understand when these seasons are over and grant me the courage to part ways with peace and love, free from conflict or misunderstanding.

I ask for Your gentle guidance in this process of discernment. May my heart be open to Your direction, and may my actions reflect Your love and grace. As I walk this path, I trust in Your plan for me, knowing that You will lead me toward relationships that are enriching and purposeful.

Thank you, Father, for Your unwavering presence in my life. I trust in Your unfailing wisdom and love to guide me in forming a Circle of relationships that honors and serves You. Amen.

section 5
LEGACY

chapter 15

WEALTH: YOUR GREATNESS ATTRACTS ABUNDANCE & PROSPERITY

Most people misunderstand what it means to have wealth. I even asked a few individuals, "What does wealth mean to you?" Not surprisingly, most of the answers surround themes of living comfortably, having an abundance of money, being rich, having stability, and other similar sentiments. Yet, this perspective, while common, barely scratches the surface of what true wealth means.

We've all heard stories about billionaires who, despite having an abundance of money, still feel an emptiness inside, or they're so consumed by the fear of losing their money, that they can't even enjoy what they have. And then, there are those with limited financial means who are deeply satisfied with life, surrounded by love, and feel spiritually affluent. So, when we speak of legacy, how much does it truly relate to being rich? And when we consider wealth, how deeply is it tied to simply having disposable income?

WEALTH BEYOND MATERIAL RICHES

While wealth in the traditional sense is predominantly tied to financial metrics—in fact, the dictionary describes it as "an abundance of valuable possessions or money"—this perspective only captures a fraction of what true wealth entails. Wealth isn't just about the money in your bank account, the brands you wear, or the size of your house. It's far more profound.

◇◇◇◇◇◇◇◇◇◇◇◇◇◇◇◇◇◇◇◇◇◇◇◇◇◇◇◇◇◇◇◇◇

True wealth is found in the richness of your inner world—it's the abundance of joy that permeates your daily life, the wealth of meaningful relationships, and the sense of fulfillment from your contributions.

True wealth is found in the richness of your inner world—it's the abundance of joy that permeates your daily life, the wealth of meaningful relationships, and the sense of fulfillment from your contributions. It resides in the heart-stirring experiences, the breathtaking moments, and the connections with people that add immeasurable value to life. This broader, more holistic view of wealth challenges us to look beyond material possessions and to appreciate the wealth of our experiences, emotions, and relationships.

On the contrary, being rich is about accumulation. It's a numerical game, often driven by societal benchmarks and external validations. While there's nothing wrong with striving for financial success, it becomes problematic when it's seen as the sole measure of a person's worth or happiness. A rich person can afford expensive things, go on extravagant vacations, and perhaps even influence others with their affordable possessions. However, without a profound sense of purpose or connection, such possessions and experiences can still feel empty.

Living life at the Pinnacle of Greatness requires you to redefine your understanding of wealth. Your Greatness attracts abundance and prosperity not just in the form of material riches but in love, joy, experiences, and connections. But it goes even deeper than that. The Bible sheds light on this breakthrough revelation in Proverbs 10:22 (NIV), which says, "The blessing of the Lord brings wealth, without painful toil for it." As if that's not a reason to get excited! God is telling us that true wealth and divine blessings flow effortlessly into our lives, and it doesn't take the burdensome stress or effort typically associated with gaining worldly riches. It's not your hustle that will sustain you. Being rich can be quite temporary—here today, gone tomorrow. But true sustainable wealth—prosperity and abundance—comes directly from the blessings and favor received from God.

First Timothy 6:17 counsels against placing hope in unstable material wealth, instead urging us to trust in God's provision for our joy, which tells us that real wealth lies in valuing life's genuine treasures. It's about valuing time over money, relationships over transactions, and purpose over possessions. A wealthy person understands that material possessions are transient, but the legacy they leave through their actions and relationships is everlasting. They prioritize mental and emotional well-being and seek to live a purpose-driven life rooted in God's orchestrated plan for them. When we align ourselves with God's vision for our lives, we attract blessings that define meaningful legacy. This spiritual wealth is what legacy truly represents. It's the wealth we should actively pursue.

GENERATIONAL WEALTH: BEYOND THE MISCONCEPTIONS

The term "generational wealth" is often misunderstood and, in many ways, it's a misleading phrase. The conventional belief is that if we leave stacks of money for our future lineage, we've set them up for success. "They won't have to struggle like I did," is how we justify the need to ensure our great-grandchildren live comfortably. But here's the crux: leaving money behind doesn't equate to leaving wealth. At best, it's providing a cushion, a safety net, perhaps even just a temporary relief. The most enduring prosperity is passed down when we instill in our children a deep respect and reverence for God, teaching them to seek His guidance and provision rather than relying solely on material inheritances that parents leave behind.

On a plane ride, I found myself engrossed in a TED Talk featuring Bill and Melinda Gates. They spoke passionately about their financial plans, highlighting how they contribute more than half of their earnings to philanthropic ventures aimed at advancing the world. What struck me most was when they showed their family photo and emphasized their decision not to leave their earnings to their children. To put this in perspective, in the Forbes 400 list of wealthiest Americans in 2023, Gates was ranked sixth with a net worth of $111 billion.

Despite these financial profits, Bill was very intentional in saying that he and Melinda have no plans of passing down riches to their children.[14] Instead, their children must discover their own "who, what, and why" to be remembered by. They believe their children should navigate their own path to purpose and impact. For the Gates family, legacy doesn't lie in just assets or inheritance but in involving their children in their mission, educating them about generosity, and

---

14 Bill and Melinda Gates, "Why Giving Away Our Wealth Has Been the Most Satisfying Thing We've Done," *TED: Ideas Worth Spreading*, Mar. 2014, www.ted.com/talks/bill_and_melinda_gates_why_giving_away_our_wealth_has_been_the_most_satisfying_thing_we_ve_done/transcript?language=en.

cultivating in them a passion for understanding how philanthropy can reshape our world.

◇◇◇◇◇◇◇◇◇◇◇◇◇◇◇◇◇◇◇◇◇◇◇◇◇◇◇◇◇◇◇◇◇◇◇

The real power and essence of generational wealth lie not in the coins, assets, or properties passed down but in the richness of understanding, the lessons shared, and the empowerment of each generation to build, nurture, and grow their own wealth.

Bill and Melinda got it right! Legacy goes beyond material wealth. It's about the richness of faith and purpose we instill in our lineage. The real power and essence of generational wealth lie not in the coins, assets, or properties passed down but in the richness of understanding, the lessons shared, and the empowerment of each generation to build, nurture, and grow their own wealth.

The saying "Give a man a fish, and you feed him for a day. Teach a man to fish, and you feed him for a lifetime" encapsulates a profound principle about legacy and sustainability. When you give someone a fish, you provide an immediate solution to their hunger, but it's a temporary fix. The next day, they'll be hungry again and will need another fish. However, teaching someone to fish equips them with a skill, a means to sustain themselves independently. The real deception in how most people classify generational wealth lies in the belief that leaving a monetary inheritance can substitute the invaluable lesson of teaching someone to fish instead of simply handing them one.

A broader understanding of generational wealth is also vividly illustrated in 1 Kings 2:2-3 (AMP), where King David offers profound advice to his son Solomon, which goes far beyond the transfer of riches or power:

> *I am going the way of all the earth [as dust to dust]. Be strong and show yourself a man; and keep the charge of the LORD your God: to walk in His ways, to keep His statutes, His commandments, His judgments, and His testimonies, as it is written in the Law of Moses, that you may prosper in all that you do and wherever you turn.*

David's counsel is an example of true generational wealth. He doesn't simply hand over his kingdom; he passes down a legacy of righteousness, obedience to God, and moral fortitude. David understands that the real treasure lies not in the kingdom itself but in living a life aligned with God's will. This alignment, he assures, is the key to true prosperity and success.

◇◇◇◇◇◇◇◇◇◇◇◇◇◇◇◇◇◇◇◇◇◇◇◇◇◇◇◇◇◇◇◇

Generational wealth is a legacy of capability, not just currency.

Generational wealth is a legacy of capability, not just currency. It's about ensuring that each successive generation is not just surviving but thriving. It's about passing down a legacy of faith, character, and divine purpose. It's teaching future generations to walk in a manner that honors their values and beliefs, ensuring not just their financial stability but their spiritual and moral richness as well. This kind of legacy fosters a cycle of prosperity that transcends time and financial measures, rooting future generations in principles that lead to sustained success and fulfillment.

So, as you plan this part of your legacy, leaving something of value for your children, their children, and generations beyond, think about this: If the true aim is the long-term stability and prosperity of your descendants, how does simply leaving behind money empower them to sustain and multiply that legacy? Does it equip them with the mindset, skills, and values to not just maintain but enhance the momentum? What are you doing today to teach them to fish for themselves?

SAVAGE SPIRITUALIST SECRETS FROM NEKEYA

Nekeya Nunn, my mentor, coach, and sponsor, also known as The Savage Spiritualist, has been an invaluable friend in my self-discovery journey. I met Nekeya at a time when entrepreneurship was far from my mind. It was her insight and belief in me, recognizing potential I hadn't yet seen in myself, that propelled me into becoming an entrepreneur. Our paths crossed while working together during a labor relations campaign, sparking an instant connection. I found myself instantly captivated by Nekeya's extraordinary success as a Black female entrepreneur, especially her dominance in the labor relations sector, a field where women who look like us traditionally didn't lead.

Beyond just leading, Nekeya scaled her company impressively—reaching $1 million in revenue by the third year, $3 million by the fifth, $5 million by the eighth, and achieving a 40 percent annual revenue increase before completing a decade in business. However, it's not just her financial success that defines her as a powerhouse. Nekeya's true wealth lies in her spiritual depth, which she credits as the cornerstone of her prosperous and abundant life.

I'll now reveal a few "Savage Spiritualist Secrets" that have significantly shaped my understanding of an abundance mindset, particularly in the realms of money, wealth, and abundance. Savage Spiritualist Secrets are a collection of profound insights and wisdom, imparted to me by Nekeya. These secrets stand out not just for their depth but for their unconventional approach. Nekeya's guidance often defies traditional thinking, offering a fresh, sometimes startling perspective on life, success, and personal growth. Her advice, while deeply insightful, doesn't shy away from being direct, bold, and unapologetically honest—traits that truly embody the "savage" aspect of her spiritual mentorship.

SAVAGE SECRET #1: MONEY ATTAINMENT IS A MINDSET

During one of our enlightening conversations, Nekeya shared an insight that deeply transformed my understanding of wealth and abundance. We had been delving into the realms of faith and belief when she revealed a profound truth: "God won't go against your own belief about yourself." This statement resonated with me on multiple levels. If you harbor a deep-seated belief that you are destined to remain in financial hardship, that belief acts like a self-fulfilling prophecy, attracting circumstances that align with it. This isn't just about positive thinking; it's about the fundamental law of attraction.

Nekeya's wisdom implies that if we believe in scarcity, scarcity is what we manifest. Conversely, if we nurture a mindset of abundance, believing in our potential to prosper and succeed, we open ourselves to opportunities and blessings in alignment with that belief. It underscores the spiritual principle that faith and belief are instrumental in shaping our experiences, including our financial reality. This revelation isn't merely about hoping for financial abundance; it's about culti-vating a deep, unshakeable belief in our worthiness of prosperity and abundance. It's a call to align our mindset with the abundance that God desires for us, understanding that our beliefs are powerful catalysts in manifesting the life we envision.

◇◇◇◇◇◇◇◇◇◇◇◇◇◇◇◇◇◇◇◇◇◇◇◇◇◇◇◇◇◇◇◇◇

Faith and belief are instrumental in shaping our experiences, including our financial reality. This revelation isn't merely about hoping for financial abundance; it's about cultivating a deep, unshakeable belief in our worthiness of prosperity and abundance.

SAVAGE SECRET #2: MONEY LIKES TO MOVE, GIVE IT A PLACE TO GO

Nekeya enlightened me about the dynamic nature of money—it's designed to move, not to remain stagnant. She explained that many people dream of becoming millionaires, yet they rarely plan how they would utilize that wealth. The key insight here is that money needs a purpose, an assignment. It isn't attracted to idle existence in wallets or bank accounts; instead, it thrives on being actively valued and circu-lated. Money, in its essence, seeks channels where it can be effectively used and multiplied, not merely accumulated.

Nekeya decided to put her theory to the test with me. She asked me, "How much money would make you feel like you've succeeded in life?"

Now, I pose this question to you. But let me channel Nekeya's unfil-tered bluntness—don't come at me with "I just want enough to be comfortable and pay my bills." Really? What are the bills, and how much are they exactly?

"Define comfortable," she challenged me, "So if I handed you that magic number right now, could you tell me where every single dollar would go? Here's a paper, write it down, spell it out."

Her point hit home hard! And with a bit of her savage flair, she explained, "By the time you've allocated for a house, car, charity, and whatever else, you'll realize you haven't even scratched the surface of those millions most people believe would make life 'comfortable.' That's why that money isn't knocking on your door—you haven't given it a clear enough reason to. Every dollar you desire needs a job, an assignment, not just a vague invitation to hang out in your bank account."

She was right. When I started drafting my list, I quickly realized I couldn't even complete it. There was nowhere for all that money I *thought* I needed to go. This exercise unveiled a common blind spot: many of us fixate on a certain amount of money without having a clear plan for it. Why would it gravitate toward us if we didn't even know what we'd do with it? It's like inviting a guest over without having any idea of how to entertain them.

I invite you now to try this exercise. Picture the amount of money you feel would equate to financial success. Then, meticulously map out how you would spend each portion of it. You may find, just as I did, that a lack of a clear plan could be what's limiting your financial abundance. It's a powerful realization to uncover what you'd do if that money landed in your lap today. If your mind isn't prepared for wealth and you lack a plan for it, the money will quickly slip away. It's vital to give it a purpose, an assignment that truly resonates with who you are.

SAVAGE SECRET #3: MONEY IS IMPARTIAL

People often mistakenly believe that their "goodness"—whether it's manifest through worship, prayer, charity, or tithes—entitles them to financial blessings, but this is a common misconception. Money, in its nature, is impartial and has no respect for personal virtues or vices. Financial abundance can be found among both the ethical and the unethical, indicating that money does not inherently gravitate toward moral righteousness or corruption.

Wealth is not a reward for good behavior or a punishment for bad deeds; it is a neutral resource that flows toward opportunities and intentions, regardless of the personal qualities of those who seek it. This reality points to the fact that money moves to where it is purposefully directed and called rather than to individuals based on their character.

Put simply, if someone is engaged in criminal activities and acquires money through illicit means yet firmly believes, without any doubt, in their success, they are likely to see that belief materialize. Conversely, a person who leads an honest life and upholds good moral values but harbors doubt about their financial prosperity will likely struggle to attain wealth. Money is drawn to where it is intended to be utilized and to those who firmly believe in their ability to acquire it. It responds to the certainty and clarity of purpose, regardless of the individual's moral compass. Goodness doesn't dictate financial status; it's about belief. If you resonate with struggle, poverty, or lack, that's what you'll attract. Believing in your worth and ability to attract wealth is key; without it, you may remain good yet financially unfulfilled.

ASK, AND IT SHALL BE GIVEN

Understanding your desires, acknowledging God's presence, and affirming a "yes" to an abundant life are important. However, without explicitly asking God for what you want, even the strongest faith may not lead to abundance. The key is making your requests known to God through direct prayer. The Bible explicitly states that abundance is a gift from the Lord, as reflected in 2 Corinthians 9:8 (AMP):

> *And God is able to make all grace [every favor and earthly blessing] come in abundance to you, so that you may always [under all circumstances, regardless of the need] have complete sufficiency in everything [being completely self-sufficient in Him] and have an abundance for every good work and act of charity.*

If abundance is a blessing that comes from God, as stated in Scripture, it stands to reason that we must turn to Him to ask for it.

◇◇◇◇◇◇◇◇◇◇◇◇◇◇◇◇◇◇◇◇◇◇◇◇◇◇◇◇◇◇◇◇◇◇◇◇◇

If abundance is a blessing that comes from God, as stated in Scripture, it stands to reason that we must turn to Him to ask for it.

This act of asking is clearly outlined in the Bible, particularly in Matthew 7:7 (NIV), which states, "Ask and it will be given to you; seek and you will find; knock and the door will be opened to you." This verse powerfully conveys the principle that by actively asking, seeking, and knocking, we open ourselves to receiving the abundance and provisions that God has in store for us.

God is eagerly waiting to hear from you, to be acknowledged as the source of all your provisions, especially in times of need. He invites us to turn to Him, to make our requests known without worry or hesitation. As Philippians 4:6 (AMP) instructs, "Do not be anxious *or* worried about anything, but in everything [every circumstance and situation] by prayer and petition with thanksgiving, continue to make your [specific] requests known to God." He is ready and willing to fulfill His promises to you, providing not just for your material needs but also offering peace that surpasses all understanding.

ALIGNING YOUR ASKS WITH GOD'S WILL

Abundance isn't about the pursuit of money, wealth, fame, or self-serving desires. It's not about praying for financial gain to ensure personal comfort or to acquire material possessions. True abundance is about having the means to fulfill a purpose that aligns with God's plan, particularly for the people He aims to reach through you. The intentions behind our prayers should be focused on positioning ourselves to further expand His ministry.

The Word shows us this principle in the story of Solomon (1 Kings 3: 6-15). When given the chance to ask anything from God, Solomon chose wisdom and understanding to better perform his God-given duties. His request greatly pleased God and led Him to bless Solomon abundantly—not just with wisdom but also with wealth and honor. Specifically, God said to Solomon in verses 11-13 (AMP):

> *"Because you have asked this and have not asked for yourself*
> *a long life nor for wealth, nor for the lives of your enemies,*

but have asked for yourself understanding to recognize justice, behold, I have done as you asked. I have given you a wise and discerning heart (mind), so that no one before you was your equal, nor shall anyone equal to you arise after you. I have also given you what you have not asked, both wealth and honor, so that there will not be anyone equal to you among the kings, for all your days."

When we align our desires with God's plan and purpose, He not only grants our prayers but often blesses us beyond our initial ask. Solomon's story shows us the importance of the intention behind our requests and the extraordinary ways God can respond to them.

◇◇◇◇◇◇◇◇◇◇◇◇◇◇◇◇◇◇◇◇◇◇◇◇◇◇◇◇◇◇◇◇◇

When we align our desires with God's plan and purpose, He not only grants our prayers but often blesses us beyond our initial ask.

THE PRAYER OF JABEZ

Bruce Wilkinson's concise yet impactful ninety-two-page book, *The Prayer of Jabez*[15], fundamentally altered my approach to petitioning God through prayer. This book centers around a brief but powerful prayer mentioned in the Bible, specifically found in 1 Chronicles 4:10. Jabez, only mentioned briefly in the Bible, is notable for his impactful

---

15 Bruce Wilkinson, *The Prayer of Jabez* (Vereeniging, South Africa: Christian Art Publishing, 2010).

prayer and the direct response it elicits from God, though the Scriptures provide little detail about his life beyond this. Jabez prays to God to bless him indeed, expand his borders, have His hand with him, and keep him from evil so that he may not cause pain. God's positive response to his prayer—"And God granted his request"—highlights the power of prayer and faith in God's willingness to bless and aid those who call upon Him.

Despite its brevity, Jabez's prayer carries a depth of intention we can model in our lives. Let's explore the powerful impact of this concise four-line prayer and discover how we can make our requests to God more meaningful, aligning them with our divine purpose. Starting with the first line, I'll paraphrase:

LINE 1: "OH, THAT YOU WOULD INDEED BLESS ME"

Jabez's request for a blessing is a plea for God's favor and goodness in his life. God's abundance is only limited by us, not by His resources, power, or willingness to give. Jabez's story illustrates how he was blessed because he placed no limit above God's nature to bless. His inclusion in the Bible demonstrates that it's not about our background or perceived destiny but about knowing who we want to be and actively asking for it.

LINE 2: "AND ENLARGE MY TERRITORY!"

Enlarging your territory means expanding your life's impact for God. It's about growing beyond our current boundaries—seeking a broader scope to serve and reach more people. When you align your business or endeavors with God's ways, it's not only appropriate to ask for growth, but He also anticipates your request for expansion. Your business or sphere of influence is the "territory" God entrusts us with. He desires for us to use it to positively impact the larger world for His glory. Asking God to enlarge our opportunities aligns with His joy to achieve great things through us.

LINE 3: "THAT YOUR HAND WOULD BE WITH ME"

Jabez asks for God's presence and guidance. This implies a desire for God's direction, support, and assurance of His involvement in every aspect of his life. Trusting in God's hand is about believing in His power to navigate through what seems impossible. Venture into something large enough that failure is guaranteed unless God steps in. Embracing challenges that feel larger than yourself aligns with serving a God greater than any of us. So, don't be afraid to tackle activities so ambitious that success is only possible with God's intervention. Life in God's service isn't about comfort but about total commitment and entrusting control to Him for success beyond our reach. God eagerly awaits our request for the supernatural power He offers.

LINE 4: "AND YOU WOULD KEEP ME FROM EVIL SO THAT IT DOES NOT HURT ME!"

Wilkinson poses a question in his book:

When was the last time you asked God to keep you away from temptation? In the same way that God wants you to ask for more blessing, more territory, and more power, He longs to hear you plead for safekeeping from evil.[16]

Jabez's is a shift from the simple prayer of "God be with me" to the proactive "God, steer me away from evil." Requesting to be kept away from evil is crucial because spiritual success often attracts negative counterforces. Typically, prayers focus on strength to endure temptation, but it's equally important to ask God to help us avoid it altogether.

16 Bruce Wilkinson, *The Prayer of Jabez*, 67.

God anticipates our requests for protection from evil and is ready to provide that safeguarding.

WRITE YOUR JABEZ PRAYER

I encourage you to take these four powerful lines from the Jabez Prayer and craft your own personal version. Make it a daily petition to God, as I have done. I even went as far as printing out my prayer and framing it on my desk, ensuring I recite it every day. This practice has been transformative for me, witnessing God move in my life in unprecedented ways.

Remember, the essence of the Jabez Prayer is about seeking expansion and abundance in areas God has called you to. In my prayer, for instance, I asked God to amplify my influence so that more people can realize their divine purpose as greatness. This very prayer led to the conception of this book—an idea that hadn't occurred to me before. As I've written each chapter, the words have flowed effortlessly, a testament to the prayer's impact. I am confident that this book is changing lives for every reader, is a best-seller, and will be translated into several languages, achieving widespread recognition and reach. How am I so certain of this, you might wonder? Because this book is a product of God's blessing, He is continually enlarging my territory, His hand is forever with me, and He is keeping evil far from me. If God could do this for Jabez—and for me—He can certainly do it for you. Write your own Jabez Prayer, tailor it to your life's calling, and watch the power of God work wonders in your journey.

chapter 16

SUCCESS: YOUR GREATNESS LEADS TO A LIFE WELL-LIVED

*D*eath is a universal inevitability, the one certainty in every life. Yet, our physical departure from this world doesn't mark the end of our influence. This is where the concept of legacy becomes vital. A legacy is life after physical death. It's about creating a life that outlives our lifespan, extending beyond the boundaries of our earthly existence.

Legacy isn't confined to what we leave for our family; it's broader and more enduring. It's about the imprint we leave on the world, the positive changes we instigate, and the lives we touch. This lasting legacy ensures that, even when we're gone, people continue to talk about our impact. They thank us in their memories and reflections as they experience the lasting effects of our contributions.

IDENTITY AS A LEGACY

In discussing legacy, we must consider the lasting power of a name. It's through our names that we are remembered and identified long after we've departed. In this digital age, our names can be searched, allowing future generations to discover who we were and what we stood for. This virtual immortality through our names is a key aspect of the legacy we leave behind. Our names become synonymous with our actions and values, transforming into a currency of their own. This currency isn't monetary; it's about recognition, respect, and the continuing impact tied to our identity.

Consider the fashion industry, for example. Names like Dior, Versace, and Gucci aren't just brands; they are legacies. These names have transcended their origins to embody style, luxury, and innovation. Their influence persists, shaping the industry and inspiring people, long after the personal stories of their founders have faded from public memory. This phenomenon raises an important question: what leads to the lasting impact of a name? Interestingly, while many of us recognize these names as iconic brands, we often know little about the personal lives of the individuals behind them.

Take Christian Dior, for instance. While the name Dior is universally recognized in the world of fragrance and fashion, the personal details of Dior's life, such as his appearance, marital status, or where he lived, are less known. Yet, these details don't diminish the power and recognition of the Dior name. People know the name Dior not just as a brand but as a symbol of excellence in the beauty and fashion industries. This recognition extends beyond his personal life and continues to thrive long after his passing. Dior died almost seventy years ago, but his name lives on, still alive on product labels, in fashion shows, and on store shelves around the world. It's a name that speaks to his legacy of innovation and elegance, a legacy that has outlasted his lifespan.

◇◇◇◇◇◇◇◇◇◇◇◇◇◇◇◇◇◇◇◇◇◇◇◇◇◇◇◇◇◇◇◇

True impact and a memorable legacy are not about what we do for ourselves but about how we positively influence and impact the lives around us.

The Bible clearly teaches that lasting legacies are built upon the foundation of Christ, and this is further emphasized in 1 Peter 4:10 (ESV): "As each has received a gift, use it to serve one another, as good stewards of God's varied grace." This scripture highlights the importance of using our unique, God-given talents and abilities not for self-glorification but for serving others. True impact and a memorable legacy are not about what we do for ourselves but about how we positively influence and impact the lives around us. Whether our actions are remembered positively or negatively, it's the extent of their reach and the lives they touch that truly matter. Since our purpose is divinely established by God, discovering and living out this God-designed life is essential in creating a meaningful, lasting legacy. By serving others with the gifts we've been given, we extend our influence and leave an enduring mark in the world.

CLAIM YOUR DIGITAL SPACE

In the digital age, one of the most effective ways to build and control your legacy is by owning your narrative online. A simple yet profound step in this direction is purchasing a domain with your name. If it's available, secure it. For me, that looks like this: www.lashawndavis.me. This domain becomes a personal space where you can start telling your story and leave digital footprints that define your identity and purpose. Start a blog, or newsletter, post updates about your life, showcase your creative work—be it photos, artwork, or writings. This is your platform to express what matters to you, the aspects of your life and work you wish to be remembered for.

This online space doesn't need to be elaborate or professionally designed. Its existence is what matters. It's a platform where you can begin to own your narrative in a space that will likely outlast you. Through this personal website, you can share your stories of impact on others, your thoughts, and your journey. It's a place to document who you are and how you want to be remembered. It's crucial to understand that this domain—your name's domain—is not about business or commerce. It's a "you" website. This space is dedicated to showcasing who you are, not what you sell or offer professionally. It's about leaving a trail of your personal journey, sharing stories of the lives you've touched and the difference you've made.

Over the years, as you grow and evolve, so will this digital space. It becomes a living archive, a testament to your journey and evolution. Long after you're gone, this domain, this piece of the digital universe that you've claimed, will remain. It will continue to tell your story, share your passions, and reflect the legacy you've built.

FOCUS ON WHAT MATTERS

In 2005, after being diagnosed with a rare form of pancreatic cancer, Steve Jobs delivered a thoughtful speech at Stanford University, reflecting on life, death, and the urgency of authentic living. He high-lighted how knowing we still have life influences our life decisions, stating, "Remembering that I'll be dead soon . . . helps me make the big choices in life . . . leaving only what is truly important." Coming a year after his diagnosis, his words highlighted death's role in clarifying life's priorities. This perspective can guide us in shaping our legacies with intention. By focusing on actions of lasting value—through creation, service, or knowledge sharing—we forge legacies that mirror our deepest principles and contributions.

As we think about these insights from Jobs and the concept of legacy, it's important to turn inward and reflect on our own lives. Ask yourself: *What are the things I do that feel meaningful? Do these activities align with the legacy I want to leave? Am I making choices based on my own values and aspirations, or am I trying to meet someone else's standards?* It's easy to get lost in the noise of everyday life, to become ensnared in pursuits that may not align with our deeper purpose.

This self-reflection is crucial. It's about understanding that every day, every hour, is a chance to build something lasting. Are you using your time to create, help, inspire, or improve? Are you living authentically, making choices that reflect your calling and not just what others expect of you?

LEGACY INHIBITORS: PRIDE, EMBARRASSMENT, AND FEAR OF FAILURE

In his speech, Jobs also shared, "Because almost everything—all external expectations, all pride, all fear of embarrassment or failure—these things just fall away in the face of death." This statement under-lines that often, our pursuit of what matters is stalled by concerns like pride, fear of embarrassment, and fear of failure. Jobs says these worries lose their significance in the grand scheme of life, especially when confronted with a deadline of our own death. The issues causing these emotions are transient and insignificant once we're gone. So, it raises the question: why do we allow such fears to wield so much power over our life choices and destiny?

Pride, especially in its haughty form—characterized by self-importance and a dismissive attitude toward others—is a major obstacle in creating a legacy. The Bible specifically warns against this kind of pride, as highlighted in Proverbs 16:18 (AMP): "Pride goes before destruction, and a haughty spirit before a fall." This scripture emphasizes the dangers of making life solely about you and the self-destructive path it leads to. To build a meaningful and positive legacy, it's essential to cultivate humility and a genuine concern for others. By prioritizing humility and service over self-centeredness, we can ensure that our actions and achievements have a positive and lasting impact.

◇◇◇◇◇◇◇◇◇◇◇◇◇◇◇◇◇◇◇◇◇◇◇◇◇◇◇◇◇◇

To build a meaningful and positive legacy, it's essential to cultivate humility and a genuine concern for others.

Personal struggles, such as guilt and embarrassment, are opportunities for meaningful impact. By overcoming these feelings instead of letting them paralyze us, we seize the opportunity to positively influence those who might benefit from our journey. These experiences equip us to extend the same comfort to others facing similar battles. This is affirmed in 2 Corinthians 1:4 (AMP):

Who comforts and encourages us in every trouble (calamity and affliction) so that we may also be able to comfort and encourage those who are in any kind of trouble or distress, with the comfort with which we ourselves are comforted by God.

By overcoming these struggles with God's help, our victories transform into tools for helping others overcome their own challenges, laying the foundation for a legacy that extends beyond our own lives.

Many people hold back from living authentically due to the fear of making mistakes. While the dread of failure can be paralyzing, the notion that actively seeking failure is a prerequisite for success is equally misguided. Understanding failure from a different perspective is key to building a legacy that is impactful, meaningful, and resonates with the lives of others.

FAILURE HAS NOTHING TO DO WITH SUCCESS

The idea that failure is a necessary precursor to success is one I find debatable. Often, failure is celebrated as a positive force, seen as a driver for perseverance, a teacher of valuable lessons, and evidence of effort. This perspective suggests that failure is something beneficial. However, I challenge this notion. By labeling failure as beneficial, we fundamentally misconstrue its meaning. Failure, by definition, is a lack of success—therefore, success is entirely absent. Yet, societal conditioning has led us to inflate the concept of failure as something more than it is, even perceiving it as a good thing related to success.

However, you must train your mindset to understand that even without achieving an intended outcome or result, you are still successful, especially when considering the power of mindset and what the Word of God says about failure.

◇◇◇◇◇◇◇◇◇◇◇◇◇◇◇◇◇◇◇◇◇◇◇◇◇◇◇◇◇◇◇◇

Train your mindset to understand that even without achieving an intended outcome or result, you are still successful.

As a believer, you should hold the conviction that there is no failure with God. This belief was powerfully embodied by my husband Victor during his pharmacy school days, shown by his tattoo bearing the letters F I N A O—Failure Is Not An Option. He adopted a mindset that completely rejected the concept of failure. This shift in thinking is about prophetically aligning your life with your thoughts and words. If you firmly tell yourself you will not fail and believe it, then failure becomes an impossibility. Victor lived this philosophy; he didn't just dismiss failure as an outcome, he refused to acknowledge its existence. Despite numerous challenges that others might label as failures, he never accepted them as such. His unwavering mindset and faith were vindicated when he not only graduated from pharmacy school but also became a licensed pharmacist in two states.

The Word of God teaches us that failure isn't a part of our journey. Scriptures, like Psalms 55:22 (AMP), reinforce the idea that with God's support, failure is not a reality for the righteous. It says, "Cast your burden on the LORD [release it], and He will sustain and uphold you; He will never allow the righteous to be shaken (slip, fall, fail)." What

He will never allow cannot happen. When we lay our challenges and plans at His feet, He not only supports us but also ensures that we do not falter or fail. It's a powerful reminder that God guarantees our stability and success, making failure an impossibility.

Understanding that failure is impossible with God, how, then, should we view an unsuccessful outcome? This is where the power of mindset becomes crucial. When we align our thoughts with this scriptural truth, our perception of "failure" changes. Things not working out favorably isn't seen as a setback but rather as a different path or a learning opportunity. This mindset, rooted in faith and positive belief, allows us to redefine our experiences not as failures but as integral steps in our journey, guided and blessed by God.

Consider Romans 8:28 (AMP):

And we know [with great confidence] that God [who is deeply concerned about us] causes all things to work together [as a plan] for good for those who love God, to those who are called according to His plan and purpose.

If all things work together for our good, as promised, then how can anything that deviates from our plans be considered as failure? As believers, we must grasp that when our plans, not in line with God's, don't succeed, it's not a failure. Could it not be God's grace redirecting us away from something that doesn't serve His purpose? Sometimes, our missteps or setbacks are simply God's way of intervening to realign us with His plan.

Outcomes, when aligned with God's purpose, are successful, irrespective of how they align with our initial expectations. Anchoring our faith in God's plan means trusting that any unintended outcome is merely a pivot to achievable success. It may be a deviation from our original expectations, but it should never be labeled as a failure. If the fear of failure has been holding you back, remember that moving in alignment with God ensures that you cannot fail. This truth should liberate you to act boldly in your faith. How you conceptualize failure is a testament of your faith and trust in God. It's in this divine alignment that you begin to create your legacy.

◇◇◇◇◇◇◇◇◇◇◇◇◇◇◇◇◇◇◇◇◇◇◇◇◇◇◇◇◇◇◇◇◇

Outcomes, when aligned with God's purpose, are successful, irrespective of how they align with our initial expectations.

WRITE YOUR OBITUARY

When I had the task of writing my grandmother's obituary after she passed away, it was an emotional journey filled with smiles, laughter, and tears as I recalled moments that defined her life for her friends and loved ones. However, I realized a gap when it came to her younger years—my knowledge was limited. While I remembered what she shared, it was different from the stories others told about the impact she had on their lives. Hearing from others about the influence she had on their lives brought a new dimension to her legacy.

This experience led me to appreciate the importance of recognizing and expressing the true value of our lives, which lies not just in our personal achievements but significantly in how we affect the lives of others. It's about understanding the depth of our impact beyond our own milestones and how our actions resonate and influence those around us. This experience highlighted the importance of recognizing and expressing the true value of our lives, which lies not only in personal milestones but significantly in the impact we have on others. It's about comprehending and articulating how our actions and presence influence those around us, shaping our legacy far beyond our individual achievements. Writing her obituary caused me to appreciate the value of understanding and articulating the impact we have on others throughout our lives, not just in our later years. It highlighted the importance of not only living a life of influence but also recognizing and sharing those moments, shaping how we are remembered and the legacy we leave behind.

Obituaries are not so much writings of death as they are celebrations of life. What we read in them are the aspects and achievements that the author found most meaningful and impactful, offering a glimpse into what truly defined the person's life. But what if you took the reins and wrote your own obituary, thereby controlling the narrative of your life's story? By doing this, you're not just recounting past achievements; you're prophetically declaring what your legacy will be. It's about envisioning and asserting how you will be remembered for making a difference in the lives of others. Writing your own obituary becomes a powerful exercise in manifesting your future. It allows you to consciously make choices that align with your vision of a well-lived life, setting a clear path for the impact and legacy you aim to leave behind.

When writing your own obituary, you will want to include aspirations as though they already have happened. This reflects a forward-thinking approach and a commitment to continuing your journey with faith, trusting in God's plan. To manifest and prophetically declare a life well-lived according to God's design, there are several key considerations to guide you in this reflective exercise:

◇ Purpose and Calling: Reflect on your God-given purpose and calling. What passions, talents, or interests has God placed in your heart?

◇ Impact and Influence: Share the impact you made in the lives of others. How will people remember you in terms of the difference you've made in their lives?

◇ Values and Beliefs: What are the core values and beliefs that guide your life? How did these shape your actions and decisions? Ensure that these are evident in the narrative of your obituary.

◇ Life Milestones: While your obituary isn't just a list of achievements, including significant milestones can highlight the journey God has led you on. Choose those that are most meaningful and reflect your growth and contributions.

◇ Legacy of Faith: Because faith is central to your life, tell others how you exercised it in your actions and relationships. How did faith influence your successful outcomes?

◇ Personal Stories: Include personal anecdotes or stories that capture the essence of who you are. These stories can be powerful illustrations of your character and your journey.

Writing your own obituary in this way is not just about summarizing a life; it's about consciously crafting a narrative that reflects your deepest values, your faith, and the legacy you aspire to leave behind.

JESUS PROPHETICALLY DECLARED HIS LEGACY

In Matthew 16, Jesus prophetically declares His legacy and outlines the purpose of His life to His disciples. After Peter recognizes Jesus as the Messiah, the Son of the living God, Jesus blesses him and speaks of building His church upon this revelation. Then, significantly, Jesus begins to reveal to His disciples the necessity of His suffering, death, and resurrection in Jerusalem (Matthew 16:21). Jesus declares His purpose as serving others and giving His life as a ransom (Matthew 20:28). In John 12:47 (NIV): Jesus says, "I did not come to judge the world but to save the world." This moment is pivotal, as Jesus openly shares the central aspect of His mission on earth—His sacrificial death and resurrection, which would become the cornerstone of the Christian faith and His enduring legacy.

◇◇◇◇◇◇◇◇◇◇◇◇◇◇◇◇◇◇◇◇◇◇◇◇◇◇◇◇◇◇◇◇◇◇◇◇◇

Like Jesus, you, too, can declare the purpose of your life and the legacy you will leave.

Like Jesus, you, too, can declare the purpose of your life and the legacy you will leave. By understanding and articulating the impact you will have, particularly in serving and influencing others, you can shape the narrative of your life in a way that aligns with God's design. This act of writing your own obituary, much like Jesus declaring His path, becomes a prophetic exercise in defining and pursuing the legacy you will leave behind. This is a powerful way of living with intention, guided by the understanding of your divine purpose.

MEASURING SUCCESS THROUGH EXPRESSIONS OF GRATITUDE

Success is defined by the impact we have on others. It transcends the realm of personal accolades or materialistic gains. True success is about living a life that moves others to express gratitude for the difference we've made in their lives. This view shifts our focus from pursuing self-centered achievements to engaging in selfless service.

The measure of success is found in the frequency and sincerity with which people thank us for our influence on them—whether through support, teaching, inspiration, or love. This concept is mirrored in the business world where customer reviews often reflect the impact of their experiences. Just as people are quick to escalate concerns or express satisfaction, the essence of success is creating a positive, memorable experience of ourselves in the lives of others, compelling them to share their experiences.

It's through the sharing of these impactful experiences with friends, family, and others that a memorable legacy is built, one that transcends the span of your life. The word-of-mouth spread by those you've touched becomes the cornerstone of a legacy that lives on well beyond your physical presence. This narrative, woven by the lives you've influenced and improved, stands as the true measure of success and the enduring testament to your life's work.

Simon Sinek's concept of starting with "why" is a powerful tool in discovering purpose. Once you've identified your "why," it's crucial to further refine your purpose by asking, "What's in it for God?" This means evaluating how your actions align with pleasing God and serving His greater plan. If an endeavor doesn't align with this, it may warrant reconsideration. Living at the Pinnacle of Greatness is about aligning every aspect of your life, including your "why," with what pleases God. Striving for this alignment ensures that your actions not only fulfill your purpose but also honor the one who is the greatest.

To achieve true success and build a legacy, it's essential that our life's assignment is deeply connected to the One who assigned it. This concept mirrors the principle of fulfilling a school or work assignment: adhering to the given instructions leads to rewards. In the context of life, the reward is living at the Pinnacle of Greatness, which means embodying the best version of oneself. By aligning our actions with what God requires and desires, we not only fulfill our earthly duties but also ascend to a level of Greatness rooted in divine purpose and fulfillment.

◇◇◇◇◇◇◇◇◇◇◇◇◇◇◇◇◇◇◇◇◇◇◇◇◇◇◇◇◇◇◇◇◇

In the context of life, the reward is living at the Pinnacle of Greatness, which means embodying the best version of oneself.

Printed in the USA
CPSIA information can be obtained
at www.ICGtesting.com
JSHW011917020224
56314JS00009B/26